The Future Evolut[ion]

The Divine Life up[on Earth]

Sri Aurobindo

Compiled with a Summary and Notes by
P.B. Saint-Hilaire

LOTUS
PRESS
Twin Lakes, WI
U.S.A.

First Published in 1963

Second Edition June 1971

Third Edition 1990

Second U.S. Edition 2003
Published by Lotus Press by arrangement with Sri Aurobindo Ashram, Copyright Department, Pondicherry, India 605002.

Lotus Press, P.O. Box 325, Twin Lakes, Wisconsin 53181.
Web: www.lotuspress.com   Email: lotuspress@lotuspress.com
(800) 824-6396

Ghose, Sri Aurobindo, 1872-1950
The Future Evolution of Man.

ISBN: 0-940985-55-1

Library of Congress Control Number: 2002108806

Printed in the United States of America.

CONTENTS

PREFACE

Man today is becoming poignantly aware of his power to influence for good or evil his own destiny. At this critical moment when he questions his future, we believe it is important to present to the public the most significant passages from those books of Sri Aurobindo which deal with this problem, the future evolution of humanity.

The quotations contained in this small volume are taken from the following three works:

> *The Life Divine* (LD)
> *The Human Cycle* (HC)
> *The Synthesis of Yoga* (SY)

At the end of the volume a few notes are given explaining the terms used by Sri Aurobindo, and a bibliographical note.

Our aim will be accomplished if the reader is induced to turn to the original works.

P. B. SAINT-HILAIRE

Sri Aurobindo Ashram
Pondicherry, India
August 15, 1962

SUMMARY

impossible on earth. In fact, it would give the truest meaning to earthly existence.   11

Man's urge towards spirituality is an undeniable indication of the inner drive of the Spirit within towards emergence, its insistence towards the next step of its manifestation.   12

III. The Present Evolutionary Crisis

It is often claimed that reason is the highest faculty of man and that it has enabled him to master himself and to master Nature. Has reason really succeeded?   14

When reason applies itself to life and action it becomes partial and passionate and the servant of forces other than the pure truth.   15

Why does man have faith in reason? Because reason has a legitimate function to fulfil, for which it is perfectly adapted; and this is to justify and illumine for man his various experiences and to give him faith and conviction in holding on to the enlarging of his consciousness.   17

But reason cannot arrive at any final truth because it can neither get to the root of things nor embrace their totality. It deals with the finite, the separate, and has no measure for the all and the Infinite.   18

The limitations of reason become very strikingly apparent when it is confronted with the religious life.   19

What is religion really and essentially, and why is it outside the realm of reason?   20

Can religion then be the guide of human life? It is a fact that in ancient times society gave a pre-eminent place to religion.   21

But, on the other hand, humanity – and in particular that portion of humanity which was the standard-bearer of progress – has revolted against the predominance of religion.   22

Very often the accredited religions have opposed progress and sided with the forces of obscurity and oppression. A denial has been needed, a revolt of the oppressed human mind and heart to correct these errors and set religion right. This would not have been so if religion were the true and sufficient guide for the whole of human life.   22

IV. Standards of Conduct and Spiritual Freedom

VI. The Triple Transformation

the true Soul, and to allow it to become the guide and sovereign of the nature.

Two principal results follow this emergence: first an effective guidance and mastery which unmask and reject all that is false and obscure or all that opposes the divine realisation; then, a spontaneous influx of spiritual experiences of all kinds.

The second phase of the transformation may be called spiritual; it is an opening to an Infinity above us, an eternal Presence, a boundless Self, an infinite Existence, an infinity of Consciousness, an infinity of Bliss, an All-Power.

The spiritual change culminates in a permanent ascension from the lower consciousness to the higher consciousness, followed by an effective permanent descent of the higher nature into the lower.

A new consciousness begins to form with new forces of thought and sight, and a power of direct spiritual realisation which is more than thought or sight.

To make this new creation permanent and perfect, the very foundation of our nature of ignorance must be transfigured and a greater power, a supramental Force must intervene to accomplish that transfiguration. This is the third phase: the supramental transformation.

VII. The Ascent towards Supermind

It is difficult to conceive intellectually what the Supermind is; and to describe it, another language would be needed than the poor abstract counters of the mind.

The transition from mind to Supermind is a passage from Nature into Supernature. For that very reason it cannot be achieved by a mere effort of our mind or our unaided aspiration. Overmind and Supermind are involved and hidden in the earth-nature; but, in order that they may emerge in us, there is needed a pressure of the same powers already formulated in their full natural force on their own superconscient planes. The powers of the Superconscience must descend into us and uplift us and transform our being.

What should be the preparation for the supramental trans-

VIII. The Gnostic Being

for the freedom of the Spirit; but it will harmonise with the manifested existence and give it an unshakable foundation. For the gnostic being, to act in the world does not signify a lapse from unity.   102

The gnostic consciousness will proceed towards an integral knowledge. And that will not be a revelation or a delivery of light out of darkness, but of light out of light.   104

The joy of an intimate self-revealing diversity of the One, the multitudinous union and happy interaction within the One, will give a fully perfected sense to the gnostic life.   105

Matter will reveal itself as an instrument of the manifestation of Spirit; a new liberated and sovereign acceptance of material Nature will then be possible.   106

The body will become a faithful and capable instrument, perfectly responsive to the Spirit.   107

Health, strength, duration, bodily happiness and ease, liberation from suffering, are a part of the physical perfection which the gnostic evolution is called upon to realise.   108

A vast calm and a deep delight of the gnostic existence rise together in a growing intensity and culminate in an eternal ecstasy. In the universal phenomenon is revealed the eternal Bliss, Ananda.   110

Two questions remain to be examined, which are important for the human conception of life.   112

1) What is the place of personality in the gnostic being?   112

In the gnostic consciousness personality and impersonality are not opposing principles; they are inseparable aspects of one and the same reality.   113

What will be the nature of the gnostic person?   114

2) If there is a gnostic personality and if it is in some way responsible for its acts, what is the place of the ethical element in the gnostic nature? What is its perfection and its fulfilment?   115

The gnostic life will reconcile freedom and order. There will be an entire accord between the free expression of the individual and 'his obedience to the inherent law of the supreme and universal Truth of things.

All mental standards would disappear because their necessity would cease; the authentic law of identity with the Divine Self would have replaced them.

IX. The Divine Life upon Earth

To be wholly and integrally conscious of oneself and of all the truth of one's being is what is implied by the perfect emergence of the individual consciousness, and it is that towards which evolution tends. All being is one, and to be fully conscious means to be integrated with the consciousness of all, with the universal self and force and action.

The plenitude of this consciousness can only be attained by realising the identity of the individual self with the transcendent Self, the supreme Reality.

This realisation demands a turning of the consciousness inward. The ordinary human consciousness is turned outward and sees the surface of things only. It recoils from entering the inner depths which appear dark and where it is afraid of losing itself. Yet the entry into this obscurity, this void, this silence is only the passage to a greater existence.

Indeed, this inward-turning movement is not an imprisonment in the personal self; it is the first step towards a true universality.

The law of the divine life is universality in action, organised by an all-seeing Will, with the sense of the true oneness of all.

New powers of consciousness and new faculties will develop in the gnostic being who will use them in a natural, normal and spontaneous way both for knowledge and for action.

The life of gnostic beings might fitly be characterised as a superhuman or divine life. But it must not be confused with past and present ideas of supermanhood.

It would be a misconception to think that a life in the full
light of Knowledge would lose its charm and become an
insipid monotony. The gnostic manifestation of life would be
more full and fruitful and its interest more vivid than the
creative interest offered to us by the world of Ignorance.   132

CHAPTER I

The Human Aspiration

Man's highest aspiration – his seeking for perfection, his longing for freedom and mastery, his search after pure truth and unmixed delight – is in flagrant contradiction with his present existence and normal experience.

The earliest preoccupation of man in his awakened thoughts and, as it seems, his inevitable and ultimate preoccupation, – for it survives the longest periods of scepticism and returns after every banishment, – is also the highest which his thought can envisage. It manifests itself in the divination of Godhead, the impulse towards perfection, the search after pure Truth and unmixed Bliss, the sense of a secret immortality. The ancient dawns of human knowledge have left us their witness to this constant aspiration; today we see a humanity satiated but not satisfied by victorious analysis of the externalities of Nature preparing to return to its primeval longings. The earliest formula of Wisdom promises to be its last, – God, Light, Freedom, Immortality.

These persistent ideals of the race are at once the contradiction of its normal experience and the affirmation of higher and deeper experiences which are abnormal to humanity and only to be attained, in their organised entirety, by a revolutionary individual effort or an evolutionary general progression. To know, possess and be the divine being in an animal and egoistic consciousness, to convert our twilit or obscure physical mentality into the plenary supramental illumination, to build peace and a self-existent bliss where there is only a stress of transitory satisfactions besieged by physical pain and emotional suffering, to establish an infinite freedom in a world which presents itself as a group of mechanical necessities, to discover and realise the immortal life in a body subjected to death and constant mutation, – this is offered to us as the manifestation of God in

Matter and the goal of Nature in her terrestrial evolution. To the ordinary material intellect which takes its present organisation of consciousness for the limit of its possibilities, the direct contradiction of the unrealised ideals with the realised fact is a final argument against their validity. But if we take a more deliberate view of the world's workings, that direct opposition appears rather as part of Nature's profoundest method and the seal of her completest sanction.   LD, 1-2

Such contradiction is part of Nature's general method; it is a sign that she is working towards a greater harmony. The reconciliation is achieved by an evolutionary progress.

For all problems of existence are essentially problems of harmony. They arise from the perception of an unsolved discord and the instinct of an undiscovered agreement or unity. To rest content with an unsolved discord is possible for the practical and more animal part of man, but impossible for his fully awakened mind, and usually even his practical parts only escape from the general necessity either by shutting out the problem or by accepting a rough, utilitarian and unillumined compromise. For essentially, all Nature seeks a harmony, life and matter in their own sphere as much as mind in the arrangement of its perceptions. The greater the apparent disorder of the materials offered or the apparent disparateness, even to irreconcilable opposition, of the elements that have to be utilised, the stronger is the spur, and it drives towards a more subtle and puissant order than can normally be the result of a less difficult endeavour. The accordance of active Life with a material form in which the condition of activity itself seems to be inertia, is one problem of opposites that Nature has solved and seeks always to solve better with greater complexities; for its perfect solution would be the material immortality of a fully organised mind-supporting animal body. The accordance of conscious mind and conscious will with a form and a life in themselves not overtly self-conscious and capable at best of a

mechanical or sub-conscious will is another problem of opposites in which she has produced astonishing results and aims
always at higher marvels; for there her ultimate miracle would
be an animal consciousness no longer seeking but possessed of
Truth and Light, with the practical omnipotence which would
result from the possession of a direct and perfected knowledge.
Not only, then, is the upward impulse of man towards the
accordance of yet higher opposites rational in itself, but it is the
only logical completion of a rule and an effort that seem to be a
fundamental method of Nature and the very sense of her
universal strivings.   LD, 2-3

> *Life evolves out of Matter, Mind out of Life, because they*
> *are already involved there: Matter is a form of veiled Life,*
> *Life a form of veiled Mind. May not Mind be a form and veil*
> *of a higher power, the Spirit, which would be supramental in*
> *its nature? Man's highest aspiration would then only*
> *indicate the gradual unveiling of the Spirit within, the*
> *preparation of a higher life upon earth.*

We speak of the evolution of Life in Matter, the evolution of
Mind in Matter; but evolution is a word which merely states the
phenomenon without explaining it. For there seems to be no
reason why Life should evolve out of material elements or Mind
out of living form, unless we accept the Vedantic solution that
Life is already involved in Matter and Mind in Life because in
essence Matter is a form of veiled Life, Life is a form of veiled
Consciousness.* And then there seems to be little objection to a
farther step in the series and the admission that mental
consciousness may itself be only a form and a veil of higher
states which are beyond Mind. In that case, the unconquerable
impulse of man towards God, Light, Bliss, Freedom, Immortality presents itself in its right place in the chain as simply the
imperative impulse by which Nature is seeking to evolve beyond
Mind, and appears to be as natural, true and just as the impulse
towards Life which she has planted in certain forms of Matter

or the impulse towards Mind which she has planted in certain forms of Life. As there, so here, the impulse exists more or less obscurely in her different vessels with an ever-ascending series in the power of its will-to-be; as there, so here, it is gradually evolving and bound fully to evolve the necessary organs and faculties. As the impulse towards Mind ranges from the more sensitive reactions of Life in the metal and the plant up to its full organisation in man, so in man himself there is the same ascending series, the preparation, if nothing more, of a higher and divine life. The animal is a living laboratory in which Nature has, it is said, worked out man. Man himself may well be a thinking and living laboratory in whom and with whose conscious co-operation she wills to work out the superman, the god. Or shall we not say, rather, to manifest God? For if evolution is the progressive manifestation by Nature of that which slept or worked in her, involved, it is also the overt realisation of that which she secretly is. We cannot, then, bid her pause at a given stage of her evolution, nor have we the right to condemn with the religionist as perverse and presumptuous or with the rationalist as a disease or hallucination any intention she may evince or effort she may make to go beyond. If it be true that Spirit is involved in Matter and apparent Nature is secret God, then the manifestation of the divine himself and the realisation of God within and without are the highest and most legitimate aim possible to man upon earth.

Thus the eternal paradox and eternal truth of a divine life in an animal body, an immortal aspiration or reality inhabiting a mortal tenement, a single and universal consciousness representing itself in limited minds and divided egos, a transcendent, indefinable, timeless and spaceless Being who alone renders time and space and cosmos possible, and in all these the higher truth realisable by the lower term, justify themselves to the deliberate reason as well as to the persistent instinct or intuition of mankind.   LD, 3-4

CHAPTER II

The Place of Man in Evolution

An evolution of consciousness is the central motive of terrestrial existence. The evolutionary working of Nature has a double process: an evolution of forms, an evolution of the soul.

A spiritual evolution, an evolution of consciousness in Matter in a constant developing self-formation till the form can reveal the indwelling spirit, is...the key-note, the central significant motive of the terrestrial existence. This significance is concealed at the outset by the involution[3] of the Spirit,[1] the Divine Reality, in a dense material Inconscience; a veil of Inconscience, a veil of insensibility of Matter hides the universal Consciousness-Force[2] which works within it, so that the Energy, which is the first form the Force of creation assumes in the physical universe, appears to be itself inconscient and yet does the works of a vast occult intelligence. The obscure mysterious creatrix ends indeed by delivering the secret consciousness out of its thick and tenebrous prison; but she delivers it slowly, little by little, in minute infinitesimal drops, in thin jets, in small vibrant concretions of energy and substance, of life, of mind, as if that were all she could get out through the crass obstacle, the dull reluctant medium of an inconscient stuff of existence. At first she houses herself in forms of Matter which appear to be altogether unconscious, then struggles towards mentality in the guise of living Matter and attains to it imperfectly in the conscious animal. This consciousness is at first rudimentary, mostly a half subconscious or just conscious instinct; it develops slowly till in more organised forms of living Matter it reaches its climax of intelligence and exceeds itself in Man, the thinking animal who develops into the reasoning mental being but carries along with him even at his highest elevation the mould of original animality, the dead weight of subconscience of body, the downward pull of gravitation towards the original Inertia and Nescience, the control of an inconscient material Nature over his conscious evolution, its power for limitation, its law of difficult development, its immense force for retardation and frustration. This control by the original Inconscience over the consciousness emerging from it takes the general shape of a mentality struggling towards knowledge but itself, in what seems to be its fundamental nature, an Ignorance. Thus hampered and burdened, mental man has still to evolve out of himself the fully conscious being, a divine manhood or a spiritual and supramental supermanhood which shall be the next product of the evolution. That transition will mark the passage from the evolution in the Ignorance to a greater evolution in the Knowledge, founded and proceeding in the light of the Superconscient and no longer in the darkness of the Ignorance and Inconscience.

This terrestrial evolutionary working of Nature from Matter to Mind[5] and beyond it has a double process: there is an outward visible process of physical evolution with birth as its machinery, – for each evolved form of body housing its own evolved power of consciousness is maintained and kept in continuity by heredity; there is, at the same time, an invisible process of soul evolution with rebirth into ascending grades of form and consciousness as its machinery. The first by itself would mean only a cosmic evolution; for the individual would be a quickly perishing instrument, and the race, a more abiding collective formulation, would be the real step in the progressive manifestation of the cosmic Inhabitant, the universal Spirit:[1] rebirth is an indispensable condition for any long duration and evolution of the individual being in the earth-existence. Each grade of cosmic manifestation, each type of form that can house the indwelling Spirit, is turned by rebirth into a means for the individual soul, the psychic entity,[4] to manifest more and more of its concealed consciousness; each life becomes a step in a victory over Matter by a greater progression of consciousness in it which shall make eventually Matter itself a means for the full manifestation of the Spirit.   LD, 824-26

Man occupies the crest of the evolutionary wave. With him occurs the passage from an unconscious to a conscious evolution.

It must be observed that the appearance of human mind and body on the earth marks a crucial step, a decisive change in the course and process of the evolution; it is not merely a continuation of the old lines. Up till this advent of a developed thinking mind in Matter evolution had been effected, not by the self-aware aspiration, intention, will or seeking of the living being, but subconsciously or subliminally[6] by the automatic operation of Nature. This was so because the evolution began from the Inconscience and the secret Consciousness had not emerged sufficiently from it to operate through the self-aware participating individual will of its living creature. But in man the necessary change has been made, – the being has become awake and aware of himself; there has been made manifest in Mind its will to develop, to grow in knowledge, to deepen the inner and widen the outer existence, to increase the capacities of the nature. Man has seen that there can be a higher status of consciousness than his own; the evolutionary œstrus is there in his parts of mind and life,[5] the aspiration to exceed himself is delivered and articulate within him: he has become conscious of a soul, discovered the self and spirit. In him, then, the substitution of a conscious for a subconscious evolution has become conceivable and practicable, and it may well be concluded that the aspiration, the urge, the persistent endeavour in him is a sure sign of Nature's will for a higher way to fulfilment, the emergence of a greater status.   LD, 843

At each step one receives an intimation of what the following step will be.

Already, in what seems to be inconscient in Life, the signs of sensation coming towards the surface are visible; in moving and breathing Life the emergence of sensitive Mind is apparent and the preparation of thinking Mind is not entirely hidden, while in thinking Mind, when it develops, there appear at an early stage the rudimentary strivings and afterwards the more developed seekings of a spiritual consciousness. As plant life contains in itself the obscure possibility of the conscious animal, as the animal mind is astir with the movements of feeling and perception and the rudiments of conception that are the first ground for man the thinker, so man the mental being is sublimated by the endeavour of the evolutionary Energy to develop out of him the spiritual man, the fully conscious being, man exceeding his first material self and discoverer of his true self and highest nature.   LD, 851

The nature of the next step is indicated by the deep aspirations awakening in the human race.

...the action of evolutionary Nature in a type of being and consciousness is first to develop the type to its utmost capacity by just such a subtilisation and increasing complexity till it is ready for her bursting of the shell, the ripened decisive emergence, reversal, turning over of consciousness on itself that constitutes a new stage in the evolution. If it be supposed that her next step is the spiritual and supramental being, the stress of spirituality in the race may be taken as a sign that that is Nature's intention, the sign too of the capacity of man to operate in himself or aid her to operate the transition. If the appearance in animal being of a type similar in some respects to the ape-kind but already from the beginning endowed with the elements of humanity was the method of the human evolution, the appearance in the human being of a spiritual type re-sembling mental-animal humanity but already with the stamp of the spiritual aspiration on it would be the obvious method of Nature for the evolutionary production of the spiritual and supramental being.

It is pertinently suggested that if such an evolutionary culmination is intended and man is to be its medium, it will only be a few especially evolved human beings who will form the new type and move towards the new life; that once done, the rest of humanity will sink back from a spiritual aspiration no longer necessary for Nature's purpose and remain quiescent in its normal status. It can equally be reasoned that the human gradation must be preserved if there is really an ascent of the soul by reincarnation through the evolutionary degrees towards the spiritual summit; for otherwise the most necessary of all the intermediate steps will be lacking. It must be conceded at once that there is not the least probability or possibility of the whole human race rising in a block to the supramental level; what is suggested is nothing so revolutionary and astonishing, but only the capacity in the human mentality, when it has reached a certain level or a certain point of stress of the evolutionary impetus, to press towards a higher plane of consciousness and its embodiment in the being. The being will necessarily undergo by this embodiment a change from the normal constitution of its nature, a change certainly of its mental and emotional and sensational constitution and also to a great extent of the body-consciousness and the physical conditioning of our life and energies; but the change of consciousness will be the chief factor, the initial movement, the physical modification will be a subordinate factor, a consequence. This transmutation of the consciousness will always remain possible to the human being when the flame of the soul, the psychic[7] kindling, becomes potent in heart and mind and the nature is ready. The spiritual aspiration is innate in man; for he is, unlike the animal, aware of imperfection and limitation and feels that there is something to be attained beyond what he now is: this urge towards self-exceeding is not likely ever to die out totally in the race. The human mental status will be always there, but it will be there not only as a degree in the scale of rebirth, but as an open step towards the spiritual and supramental status.   LD, 842-43

A change of consciousness is the major fact of the next evolutionary transformation, and the consciousness itself, by its own mutation, will impose and effect any necessary mutation of the body.

In the previous stages of the evolution Nature's first care and effort had to be directed towards a change in the physical organisation, for only so could there be a change of consciousness; this was a necessity imposed by the insufficiency of the force of consciousness already in formation to effect a change in the body. But in man a reversal is possible, indeed inevitable; for it is through his consciousness, through its transmutation and no longer through a new bodily organism as a first instrumentation that the evolution can and must be effected. In the inner reality of things a change of consciousness was always the major fact, the evolution has always had a spiritual significance and the physical change was only instrumental; but this relation was concealed by the first abnormal balance of the two factors, the body of the external Inconscience outweighing and obscuring in importance the spiritual element, the conscious being. But once the balance has been righted, it is no longer the change of body that must precede the change of consciousness; the consciousness itself by its mutation will necessitate and operate whatever mutation is needed for the body. It has to be noted that the human mind has already shown a capacity to aid Nature in the evolution of new types of plant and animal; it has created new forms of its environment, developed by knowledge and discipline considerable changes in its own mentality. It is not an impossibility that man should aid Nature consciously also in his own spiritual and physical evolution and transformation. The urge to do it is already there and partly effective, though still incompletely understood and accepted by the surface mentality; but one day it may understand, go deeper within itself and discover the means, the secret energy, the intended operation of the Consciousness-Force[2] within which is the hidden reality of what we call Nature.

All these are conclusions that can be arrived at even from the observation of the outward phenomena of Nature's progression, her surface evolution of being and of consciousness in the physical birth and the body. But there is the other, the invisible factor; there is rebirth, the progress of the soul by ascent from grade to grade of the evolving existence, and in the grades to higher and higher types of bodily and mental instrumentation. In this progression the psychic[4] entity is still veiled, even in man the conscious mental being, by its instruments, by mind and life and body; it is unable to manifest fully, held back from coming to the front where it can stand out as the master of its nature, obliged to submit to a certain determination by the instruments, to a domination of Purusha by Prakriti.[8] But in man the psychic part of the personality is able to develop with a much greater rapidity than in the inferior creation, and a time can arrive when the soul entity is close to the point at which it will emerge from behind the veil into the open and become the master of its instrumentation in Nature. But this will mean that the secret indwelling spirit, the Daemon, the Godhead within is on the point of emergence; and, when it emerges, it can hardly be doubted that its demand will be, as indeed it already is in the mind itself when it undergoes the inner psychic influence, for a diviner, a more spiritual existence. In the nature of the earth life where the mind is an instrument of the Ignorance, this can only be effected by a change of consciousness, a transition from a foundation in Ignorance to a foundation in Knowledge, from the mental to a supramental consciousness, a supramental instrumentation of Nature.   LD, 843-45

There is no reason to suppose that this transformation is impossible on earth. In fact, it would give the truest meaning to earthly existence.

There is no conclusive validity in the reasoning that because this is a world of Ignorance, such a transformation can only be achieved by a passage to a heaven beyond or cannot be achieved at all and the demand of the psychic entity is itself ignorant and must be replaced by a merger of the soul in the Absolute. This conclusion could only be solely valid if Ignorance were the

whole meaning, substance and power of the world-manifesta-
tion or if there were no element in World-Nature itself through
which there could be an exceeding of the ignorant mentality
that still burdens our present status of being. But the Ignorance
is only a portion of this World-Nature; it is not the whole of it,
not the original power or creator: it is in its higher origin a self-
limiting Knowledge and even in its lower origin, its emergence
out of the sheer material Inconscience, it is a suppressed
Consciousness labouring to find, to recover itself, to manifest
knowledge, which is its true character, as the foundation of
existence. In universal Mind itself there are ranges above our
mentality which are instruments of the cosmic truth-cognition,
and into these the mental being can surely rise; for already it
rises towards them in supernormal conditions or receives from
them without yet knowing or possessing them intuitions,
spiritual intimations, large influxes of illumination or spiritual
capacity. All these ranges are conscious of what is beyond them,
and the highest of them is directly open to the Supermind,[9]
aware of the Truth-consciousness which exceeds it. Moreover,
in the evolving being itself, those greater powers of consciousness are here, supporting mind-truth, underlying its action
which screens them; this Supermind and those Truth-powers
uphold Nature by their secret presence: even, truth of mind is
their result, a diminished operation, a representation in partial
figures. It is, therefore, not only natural but seems inevitable
that these higher powers of Existence should manifest here in
Mind as Mind itself has manifested in Life and Matter.

LD, 845-46

*Man's urge towards spirituality is an undeniable indication
of the inner drive of the Spirit within towards emergence, its
insistence towards the next step of its manifestation.*

If a spiritual unfolding on earth is the hidden truth of our birth
into Matter, if it is fundamentally an evolution of consciousness
that has been taking place in Nature, then man as he is cannot

be the last term of that evolution: he is too imperfect an expression of the spirit, Mind itself, a too limited form and instrumentation; Mind is only a middle term of consciousness, the mental being can only be a transitional being. If, then, man is incapable of exceeding mentality, he must be surpassed and supermind[9] and superman must manifest and take the lead of the creation. But if his mind is capable of opening to what exceeds it, then there is no reason why man himself should not arrive at supermind and supermanhood or at least lend his mentality, life and body to an evolution of that greater term of the Spirit manifesting in Nature.   LD, 846-47

CHAPTER III

The Present Evolutionary Crisis

It is often claimed that reason is the highest faculty of man and that it has enabled him to master himself and to master Nature. Has reason really succeeded?

... apart from the stumbling action of the world, there has been a labour of the individual thinker in man and this has achieved a higher quality and risen to a loftier and clearer atmosphere above the general human thought-levels. Here there has been the work of a reason that seeks always after knowledge and strives patiently to find out truth for itself, without bias, without the interference of distorting interests, to study everything, to analyse everything, to know the principle and process of everything. Philosophy, Science, learning, the reasoned arts, all the agelong labour of the critical reason in man have been the result of this effort. In the modern era under the impulsion of Science this effort assumed enormous proportions and claimed for a time to examine successfully and lay down finally the true principle and the sufficient rule of process not only for all the activities of Nature, but for all the activities of man. It has done great things, but it has not been in the end a success. The human mind is beginning to perceive that it has left the heart of almost every problem untouched and illumined only outsides and a certain range of processes. There has been a great and ordered classification and mechanisation, a great discovery and practical result of increasing knowledge, but only on the physical surface of things. Vast abysses of Truth lie below in which are concealed the real springs, the mysterious powers and secretly decisive influences of existence. It is a question whether the intellectual reason will ever be able to give us an adequate account of these deeper and greater things or subject them to the intelligent will as it has succeeded in explaining and canalising, though still imperfectly, yet with much show of triumphant result, the forces of physical Nature. But these other powers are much larger, subtler, deeper down, more hidden, elusive and variable than those of physical Nature.

The whole difficulty of the reason in trying to govern our existence is that because of its own inherent limitations it is unable to deal with life in its complexity or in its integral movements; it is compelled to break it up into parts, to make more or less artificial classifications, to build systems with limited data which are contradicted, upset or have to be continually modified by other data, to work out a selection of regulated potentialities which is broken down by the bursting of a new wave of yet unregulated potentialities.   HC, 100-02

> *When reason applies itself to life and action it becomes*
> *partial and passionate and the servant of forces other than*
> *the pure truth.*

But even if the intellect keeps itself as impartial and disinterested as possible, – and altogether impartial, altogether disinterested the human intellect cannot be unless it is content to arrive at an entire divorce from practice or a sort of large but ineffective tolerantism, eclecticism or sceptical curiosity, – still the truths it discovers or the ideas it promulgates become, the moment they are applied to life, the plaything of forces over which the reason has little control. Science pursuing its cold and even way has made discoveries which have served on one side a practical humanitarianism, on the other supplied monstrous weapons to egoism and mutual destruction; it has made possible a gigantic efficiency of organisation which has been used on one side for the economic and social amelioration of the nations and on the other for turning each into a colossal battering-ram of aggression, ruin and slaughter. It has given rise on the one side to a large rationalistic and altruistic humanitarianism, on the other it has justified a godless egoism, vitalism, vulgar will to power and success. It has drawn mankind together and given it a new hope and at the same time crushed it with the burden of a monstrous commercialism. Nor is this due, as is so often asserted, to its divorce from religion or to any lack of idealism. Idealistic philosophy has been equally at the service of the powers of good and evil and provided an intellectual conviction both for reaction and for progress. Organised religion itself has often enough in the past hounded men to crime and massacre and justified obscurantism and oppression.

The truth is that upon which we are now insisting, that reason is in its nature an imperfect light with a large but still restricted mission and that once it applies itself to life and action it becomes subject to what it studies and the servant and counsellor of the forces in whose obscure and ill-understood struggle it intervenes. It can in its nature be used and has always been used to justify any idea, theory of life, system of society or government, ideal of individual or collective action to which the will of man attaches itself for the moment or through the centuries. In philosophy it gives equally good reasons for monism and pluralism or for any halting-place between them, for the belief in Being or for the belief in Becoming, for optimism and pessimism, for activism and quietism. It can justify the most mystic religionism and the most positive atheism, get rid of God or see nothing else. In aesthetics it supplies the basis equally for classicism and romanticism, for an idealistic, religious or mystic theory of art or for the most earthy realism. It can with equal power base austerely a strict and narrow moralism or prove triumphantly the thesis of the antinomian. It has been the sufficient and convincing prophet of every kind of autocracy or oligarchy and of every species of democracy; it supplies excellent and satisfying reasons for competitive individualism and equally excellent and satisfying reasons for communism or against communism and for State socialism or for one variety of socialism against another. It can place itself with equal effectivity at the service of utilitarianism, economism, hedonism, aestheticism, sensualism, ethicism, idealism or any other essential need or activity of man and build around it a philosophy, a political and social system, a theory of conduct and life. Ask it not to lean to one idea alone, but to make an eclectic combination or a synthetic harmony and it will satisfy you; only, there being any number of possible combinations or harmonies, it will equally well justify the one or the other and set up or throw down any one of them according as the spirit in man is attracted to or withdraws from it. For it is really that which decides and the reason is only a brilliant servant and minister of this veiled and secret sovereign.

HC, 111-12

Why does man have faith in reason? Because reason has a legitimate function to fulfil, for which it is perfectly adapted; and this is to justify and illumine for man his various experiences and to give him faith and conviction in holding on to the enlarging of his consciousness.

This truth is hidden from the rationalist because he is supported by two constant articles of faith, first that his own reason is right and the reason of others who differ from him is wrong, and secondly that whatever may be the present deficiencies of the human intellect, the collective reason will eventually arrive at purity and be able to found human thought and life securely on a clear rational basis entirely satisfying to the intelligence. His first article of faith is no doubt the common expression of our egoism and arrogant fallibility, but it is also something more; it expresses this truth that it is the legitimate function of the reason to justify to man his action and his hope and the faith that is in him and to give him that idea and knowledge, however restricted, and that dynamic conviction, however narrow and intolerant, which he needs in order that he may live, act and grow in the highest light available to him. The reason cannot grasp all truth in its embrace because truth is too infinite for it; but still it does grasp the something of it which we immediately need, and its insufficiency does not detract from the value of its work, but is rather the measure of its value. For man is not intended to grasp the whole truth of his being at once, but to move towards it through a succession of experiences and a constant, though not by any means perfectly continuous self-enlargement. The first business of reason then is to justify and enlighten to him his various experiences and to give him faith and conviction in holding on to his self-enlargings. It justifies to him now this, now that, the experiences of the moment, the receding light of the past, the half-seen vision of the future. Its inconstancy, its divisibility against itself, its power of sustaining opposite views are the whole secret of its value. It would not do indeed for it to support too conflicting views in the same individual, except at moments of awakening and transition, but in the collective body of men and in the successions of Time that is its whole business. For so man moves towards the infinity of the Truth by the experience of its variety; so his reason helps him to build, change, destroy what he has built and prepare a new construction, in a word, to progress, grow, enlarge himself in his self-knowledge and world-knowledge and their works.

HC, 112-13

But reason cannot arrive at any final truth because it can neither get to the root of things nor embrace their totality. It deals with the finite, the separate and has no measure for the all and the Infinite.

The second article of faith of the believer in reason is also an error and yet contains a truth. The reason cannot arrive at any final truth because it can neither get to the root of things nor embrace the totality of their secrets; it deals with the finite, the separate, the limited aggregate, and has no measure for the all and the infinite. Nor can reason found a perfect life for man or a perfect society. A purely rational human life would be a life baulked and deprived of its most powerful dynamic sources; it would be a substitution of the minister for the sovereign. A purely rational society could not come into being and, if it could be born, either could not live or would sterilise and petrify human existence. The root powers of human life, its intimate causes are below, irrational, and they are above, suprarational.

But this is true that by constant enlargement, purification, openness the reason of man is bound to arrive at an intelligent sense even of that which is hidden from it, a power of passive yet sympathetic reflection of the Light that surpasses it. Its limit is reached, its function is finished when it can say to man, "There is a Soul, a Self, a God in the world and in man who works concealed and all is his self-concealing and gradual self-unfolding. His minister I have been, slowly to unseal your eyes, remove the thick integuments of your vision until there is only my own luminous veil between you and him. Remove that and make the soul of man one in fact and nature with this Divine; then you will know yourself, discover the highest and widest law of your being, become the possessors or at least the receivers and instruments of a higher will and knowledge than mine and lay hold at last on the true secret and the whole sense of a human and yet divine living."   HC, 113-14

The limitations of reason become very strikingly apparent when it is confronted with the religious life.

Here is a realm at which the intellectual reason gazes with the bewildered mind of a foreigner who hears a language of which the words and the spirit are unintelligible to him and sees everywhere forms of life and principles of thought and action which are absolutely strange to his experience.

The unaided intellectual reason faced with the phenomena of the religious life is naturally apt to adopt one of two attitudes, both of them shallow in the extreme, hastily presumptuous and erroneous. Either it views the whole thing as a mass of superstition, a mystical nonsense, a farrago of ignorant barbaric survivals, – that was the extreme spirit of the rationalist now happily, though not dead, yet much weakened and almost moribund, – or it patronises religion, tries to explain its origins, to get rid of it by the process of explaining it away; or it labours gently or forcefully to reject or correct its superstitions, crudities, absurdities, to purify it into an abstract nothingness or persuade it to purify itself in the light of the reasoning intelligence; or it allows it a role, leaves it perhaps for the edification of the ignorant, admits its value as a moralising influence or its utility to the State for keeping the lower classes in order, even perhaps tries to invent that strange chimera, a rational religion.   HC, 120-21

What is religion really and essentially and why is it outside the realm of reason?

The deepest heart, the inmost essence of religion, apart from its outward machinery of creed, cult, ceremony and symbol, is the search for God and the finding of God. Its aspiration is to discover the Infinite, the Absolute, the One, the Divine, who is all these things and yet no abstraction but a Being. Its work is a sincere living out of the true and intimate relations between man and God, relations of unity, relations of difference, relations of an illuminated knowledge, an ecstatic love and delight, an absolute surrender and service, a casting of every part of our existence out of its normal status into an uprush of man towards the Divine and a descent of the Divine into man. All this has nothing to do with the realm of reason or its normal activities; its aim, its sphere, its process is suprarational. The knowledge of God is not to be gained by weighing the feeble arguments of reason for or against his existence: it is to be gained only by a self-transcending and absolute consecration, aspiration and experience. Nor does that experience proceed by anything like rational scientific experiment or rational philosophic thinking. Even in those parts of religious discipline which seem most to resemble scientific experiment, the method is a verification of things which exceed the reason and its timid scope. Even in those parts of religious knowledge which seem most to resemble intellectual operations, the illuminating faculties are not imagination, logic and rational judgment, but revelations, inspirations, intuitions, intuitive discernments that leap down to us from a plane of suprarational light. The love of God is an infinite and absolute feeling which does not admit of any rational limitations and does not use a language of rational worship and adoration; the delight in God is that peace and bliss which passes all understanding. The surrender to God is the surrender of the whole being to a suprarational light, will, power and love and his service takes no account of the compromises with life which the practical reason of man uses as the best part of its method in the ordinary conduct of mundane existence. Wherever religion really finds itself, wherever it opens itself to its own spirit, – there is plenty of that sort of religious practice which is halting, imperfect, half-sincere, only half-sure of itself and in which reason can get in a word, – its way is absolute and its fruits are ineffable.   HC, 122

> *Can religion then be the guide of human life? It is a fact that*
> *in ancient times society gave a pre-eminent place to religion.*

Since the infinite, the absolute and transcendent, the universal, the One is the secret summit of existence and to reach the spiritual consciousness and the Divine the ultimate goal and aim of our being and therefore of the whole development of the individual and the collectivity in all its parts and all its activities, reason cannot be the last and highest guide.... For reason stops short of the Divine and only compromises with the problems of life.... Where then are we to find the directing light and the regulating and harmonising principle?

The first answer which will suggest itself, the answer constantly given by the Asiatic mind, is that we shall find it directly and immediately in religion.

A certain pre-eminence of religion, the overshadowing or at least the colouring of life, an overtopping of all the other instincts and fundamental ideas by the religious instinct and the religious idea is, we may note, not peculiar to Asiatic civilisations, but has always been more or less the normal state of the human mind and of human societies.... We must suppose then that in this leading, this predominant part assigned to religion by the normal human collectivity there is some great need and truth of our natural being to which we must always after however long an infidelity return.   HC, 162-63

But, on the other hand, humanity – and in particular that portion of humanity which was the standard-bearer of progress – has revolted against the predominance of religion.

On the other hand, we must recognise the fact that in a time of great activity, of high aspiration, of deep sowing, of rich fruit-bearing, such as the modern age with all its faults and errors has been, a time especially when humanity got rid of much that was cruel, evil, ignorant, dark, odious, not by the power of religion, but by the power of the awakened intelligence and of human idealism and sympathy, this predominance of religion has been violently attacked and rejected by that portion of humanity which was for that time the standard-bearer of thought and progress, Europe after the Renascence, modern Europe.

HC, 163

Very often the accredited religions have opposed progress and sided with the forces of obscurity and oppression. And it has needed a denial, a revolt of the oppressed human mind and heart to correct these errors and set religion right. This would not have been so if religion were the true and sufficient guide of the whole of human life.

We need not follow the rationalistic or atheistic mind through all its aggressive indictment of religion. We need not for instance lay a too excessive stress on the superstitions, aberrations, violences, crimes even, which Churches and cults and creeds have favoured, admitted, sanctioned, supported or exploited for their own benefit.... As well might one cite the crimes and errors which have been committed in the name of liberty or of order as a sufficient condemnation of the ideal of liberty or the ideal of social order. But we have to note the fact that such a thing was possible and to find its explanation.... We must observe the root of this evil, which is not in true religion itself, but in its infrarational parts, not in spiritual faith and aspiration, but in our ignorant human confusion of religion with a particular creed, sect, cult, religious society or church....

The whole root of the historic insufficiency of religion as a guide and control of human society lies there. Churches and creeds have, for example, stood violently in the way of philosophy and science, burned a Giordano Bruno, imprisoned a Galileo, and so generally misconducted themselves in this matter that philosophy and science had in self-defence to turn upon Religion and rend her to pieces in order to get a free field for their legitimate development; and this because men in the passion and darkness of their vital nature had chosen to think that religion was bound up with certain fixed intellectual conceptions about God and the world which could not stand scrutiny, and therefore scrutiny had to be put down by fire and sword; scientific and philosophical truth had to be denied in order that religious error might survive. We see too that a narrow religious spirit often oppresses and impoverishes the joy and beauty of life, either from an intolerant asceticism or, as the Puritans attempted it, because they could not see that religious austerity is not the whole of religion, though it may be an important side of it, is not the sole ethico-religious approach to God, since love, charity, gentleness, tolerance, kindliness are also and even more divine, and they forgot or never knew that God is love and beauty as well as purity. In politics religion has often thrown itself on the side of power and resisted the coming of larger political ideals, because it was itself, in the form of a Church, supported by power and because it confused religion with the Church, or because it stood for a false theocracy, forgetting that true theocracy is the kingdom of God in man and not the kingdom of a Pope, a priesthood or a sacerdotal class.

So too it has often supported a rigid and outworn social system, because it thought its own life bound up with social forms with which it happened to have been associated during a long portion of its own history and erroneously concluded that even a necessary change there would be a violation of religion and a danger to its existence. As if so mighty and inward a power as the religious spirit in man could be destroyed by anything so small as the change of a social form or so outward as a social readjustment! This error in its many shapes has been the great weakness of religion as practised in the past and the opportunity and justification for the revolt of the intelligence, the aesthetic sense, the social and political idealism, even the ethical spirit of the human being against what should have been its own highest tendency and law.   HC, 164-66

If religion has failed, it is because it has confused the essential with the adventitious. True religion is spiritual religion, it is a seeking after God, the opening of the deepest life of the soul to the indwelling Godhead, the eternal Omnipresence. Dogmas, cults, moral codes are aids and props; they may be offered to man but not imposed on him.

It is true in a sense that religion should be the dominant thing in life, its light and law, but religion as it should be and is in its inner nature, its fundamental law of being, a seeking after God, the cult of spirituality, the opening of the deepest life of the soul to the indwelling Godhead, the eternal Omnipresence. On the other hand, it is true that religion when it identifies itself only with a creed, a cult, a Church, a system of ceremonial forms, may well become a retarding force and there may therefore arise a necessity for the human spirit to reject its control over the varied activities of life. There are two aspects of religion, true religion and religionism. True religion is spiritual religion, that which seeks to live in the spirit, in what is beyond the intellect, beyond the aesthetic and ethical and practical being of man, and to inform and govern these members of our being by the higher light and law of the spirit. Religionism, on the contrary, entrenches itself in some narrow pietistic exaltation of the lower members or lays exclusive stress on intellectual dogmas, forms and ceremonies, on some fixed and rigid moral code, on some religio-political or religio-social system. Not that these things are altogether negligible or that they must be unworthy or unnecessary or that a spiritual religion need disdain the aid of forms, ceremonies, creeds or systems. On the contrary, they are needed by man because the lower members have to be exalted and raised before they can be fully spiritualised, before they can directly feel the spirit and obey its law. An intellectual formula is often needed by the thinking and reasoning mind, a form or ceremony by the aesthetic temperament or other parts of the infrarational being, a set moral code by man's vital nature in their turn towards the inner life. But these things are aids and supports, not the essence; precisely because they belong to the rational and infrarational parts, they can be nothing more and, if too blindly insisted on, may even hamper the suprarational light. Such as they are, they have to be offered to man and used by him, but not to be imposed on him as his sole law by a forced and inflexible domination. In the use of them toleration and free permission of variation is the first rule which should be observed. The spiritual essence of religion is alone the one thing supremely needful, the thing to which we have always to hold and subordinate to it every other element or motive.

HC, 166-67

Moreover, religion often considers spiritual life as made up of renunciation and mortification. Religion thus becomes a force that discourages life and it cannot, therefore, be a true law and guide for life.

But here comes in an ambiguity which brings in a deeper source of divergence. For by spirituality religion seems often to mean something remote from earthly life, different from it, hostile to it. It seems to condemn the pursuit of earthly aims as a trend opposed to the turn to a spiritual life and the hopes of man on earth as an illusion or a vanity incompatible with the hopes of man in heaven. The spirit then becomes something aloof which man can only reach by throwing away the life of his lower members. Either he must abandon this nether life after a certain point, when it has served its purpose, or must persistently discourage, mortify and kill it. If that be the true sense of religion, then obviously religion has no positive message for human society in the proper field of social effort, hope and aspiration or for the individual in any of the lower members of his being. For each principle of our nature seeks naturally for perfection in its own sphere and, if it is to obey a higher power, it must be because that power gives it a greater perfection and a fuller satisfaction even in its own field. But if perfectibility is denied to it and therefore the aspiration to perfection taken away by the spiritual urge, then it must either lose faith in itself and the power to pursue the natural expansion of its energies and activities or it must reject the call of the spirit in order to follow its own bend and law, *dharma*.[10] This quarrel between earth and heaven, between the spirit and its members becomes still more sterilising if spirituality takes the form of a religion of sorrow and suffering and austere mortification and the gospel of the vanity of things; in its exaggeration it leads to such nightmares of the soul as that terrible gloom and hopelessness of the Middle Ages in their worst moment when the one hope of mankind seemed to be in the approaching and expected end of the world, an inevitable and desirable *Pralaya*.[11] But even in less pronounced and intolerant forms of this pessimistic attitude with regard to the world, it becomes a force for the discouragement of life and cannot, therefore, be a true law and guide for life. All pessimism is to that extent a denial of the Spirit, of its fullness and power, an impatience with the ways of God in the world, an insufficient faith in the divine Wisdom and Will that created the world and for ever guide it. It admits a wrong notion about that supreme Wisdom and Power and therefore cannot itself be the supreme wisdom and power of the spirit to which the world can look for guidance and for the uplifting of its whole life towards the Divine.

The world-shunning monk, the mere ascetic may indeed well find by this turn his own individual and peculiar salvation, the spiritual recompense of his renunciation and *tapasya*,[12] as the materialist may find by his own exclusive method the appropriate rewards of his energy and concentrated seeking; but neither can be the true guide of mankind and its law-giver. The monastic attitude implies a fear, an aversion, a distrust of life and its aspirations, and one cannot wisely guide that with which one is entirely out of sympathy, that which one wishes to minimise and discourage. The sheer ascetic spirit, if it directed life and human society, could only prepare it to be a means for denying itself and getting away from its own motives. An ascetic guidance might tolerate the lower activities, but only with a view to persuade them in the end to minimise and finally cease from their own action. HC, 167-68, 169

In spirituality then, restored to its true sense, we must seek for the directing light and the harmonising law.

But a spirituality which draws back from life to envelop it without being dominated by it does not labour under this disability. The spiritual man who can guide human life towards its perfection is typified in the ancient Indian idea of the Rishi,[13] one who has lived fully the life of man and found the word of the supra-intellectual, supramental, spiritual truth. He has risen above these lower limitations and can view all things from above, but also he is in sympathy with their effort and can view them from within; he has the complete inner knowledge and the higher surpassing knowledge. Therefore he can guide the world humanly as God guides it divinely, because like the Divine he is in the life of the world and yet above it.

In spirituality, then, understood in this sense, we must seek for the directing light and the harmonising law, and in religion only in proportion as it identifies itself with this spirituality. So long as it falls short of this, it is one human activity and power among others, and, even if it be considered the most important and the most powerful, it cannot wholly guide the others. If it seeks always to fix them into the limits of a creed, an unchangeable law, a particular system, it must be prepared to see them revolting from its control; for although they may accept this impress for a time and greatly profit by it, in the end they must move by the law of their being towards a freer activity and an untrammelled movement. Spirituality respects the freedom of the human soul, because it is itself fulfilled by freedom; and the deepest meaning of freedom is the power to expand and grow towards perfection by the law of one's own nature, *dharma*.[10]

HC, 169-70

On the other hand, modern man has not solved the problem of the relation of the individual to the society. What are their respective roles in the spiritual progress of mankind?

In our human aspiration towards a personal perfection and the perfection of the life of the race the elements of the future evolution are foreshadowed and striven after, but in a confusion of half-enlightened knowledge; there is a discord between the necessary elements, an opposing emphasis, a profusion of rudimentary unsatisfying and ill-accorded solutions. These sway between the three principal preoccupations of our idealism, – the complete single development of the human being in himself, the perfectibility of the individual, a full development of the collective being, the perfectibility of society, and, more pragmatically restricted, the perfect or best possible relations of individual with individual and society and of community with community. An exclusive or dominant emphasis is laid sometimes on the individual, sometimes on the collectivity or society, sometimes on a right and balanced relation between the individual and the collective human whole.... In recent times the whole stress has passed to the life of the race, to a search for the perfect society, and latterly to a concentration on the right organisation and scientific mechanisation of the life of mankind as a whole; the individual now tends more to be regarded only as a member of the collectivity, a unit of the race whose interest of the organised society, and much less or not at all as a mental or spiritual being with his own right and power of existence. This tendency has not yet reached its acme everywhere, but everywhere it is rapidly increasing and heading towards dominance.

Thus, in the vicissitudes of human thought, on one side the individual is moved or invited to discover and pursue his own self-affirmation, his own development of mind and life and body, his own spiritual perfection; on the other he is called on to efface and subordinate himself and to accept the ideas, ideals, wills, instincts, interests of the community as his own. He is moved by Nature to live for himself and by something deep within him to affirm his individuality; he is called upon by society and by a certain mental idealism to live for humanity or for the greater good of the community. The principle of self and its interest is met and opposed by the principle of altruism. The State erects its godhead and demands his obedience, submission, subordination, self-immolation; the individual has to affirm against this exorbitant claim the rights of his ideals, his ideas, his personality, his conscience. It is evident that all this conflict of standards is a groping of the mental Ignorance of man seeking to find its way and grasping different sides of the truth but unable by its want of integrality in knowledge to harmonise them together. A unifying and harmonising knowledge can alone find the way, but that knowledge belongs to a deeper principle of our being to which oneness and integrality are native. It is only by finding that in ourselves that we can solve the problem of our existence and with it the problem of the true way of individual and communal living.

There is a Reality, a truth of all existence which is greater and more abiding than all its formations and manifestations; to find that truth and Reality and live in it, achieve the most perfect manifestation and formation possible of it, must be the secret of perfection whether of individual or communal being. This Reality is there within each thing and gives to each of its formations its power of being and value of being. The universe is a manifestation of the Reality, and there is a truth of the universal existence, a Power of cosmic being, an all-self or world-spirit. Humanity is a formation or manifestation of the Reality in the universe, and there is a truth and self of humanity, a human spirit, a destiny of human life. The community is a formation of the Reality, a manifestation of the spirit of man, and there is a truth, a self, a power of the collective being. The individual is a formation of the Reality, and there is a truth of the individual, an individual self, soul or spirit that expresses itself through the individual mind, life and body and can express itself too in something that goes beyond mind, life and body, something even that goes beyond humanity. For our humanity is not the whole of the Reality or its best possible self-formation or self-expression, – the Reality has assumed before man existed an infra-human formation and self-creation and can assume after him or in him a suprahuman formation and self-creation.   LD, 1046-49

It is wrong to demand that the individual subordinate himself to the collective or merge in it, because it is by its most advanced individuals that the collectivity progresses and they can really advance only if they are free. But it is true that as the individual advances spiritually, he finds himself more and more united with the collectivity and the All.

The individual is indeed the key of the evolutionary movement; for it is the individual who finds himself, who becomes conscious of the Reality. The movement of the collectivity is a largely subconscious mass movement; it has to formulate and express itself through the individuals to become conscious: its general mass consciousness is always less evolved than the consciousness of its most developed individuals, and it progresses in so far as it accepts their impress or develops what they develop. The individual does not owe his ultimate allegiance

either to the State which is a machine or to the community
which is a part of life and not the whole life: his allegiance must
be to the Truth, the Self, the Spirit, the Divine which is in him
and in all; not to subordinate or lose himself in the mass, but to
find and express that truth of being in himself and help the
community and humanity in its seeking for its own truth and
fullness of being must be his real object of existence. But the
extent to which the power of the individual life or the spiritual
Reality within it becomes operative, depends on his own
development: so long as he is undeveloped, he has to subordinate in many ways his undeveloped self to whatever is greater
than it. As he develops, he moves towards a spiritual freedom,
but this freedom is not something entirely separate from all-
existence; it has a solidarity with it because that too is the self,
the same spirit. As he moves towards spiritual freedom, he
moves also towards spiritual oneness. The spiritually realised,
the liberated man is preoccupied, says the Gita,[14] with the good
of all beings; Buddha discovering the way of Nirvana[16] must
turn back to open that way to those who are still under the
delusion of their constructive instead of their real being, – or
non-being; Vivekananda,[15] drawn by the Absolute, feels also the
call of the disguised Godhead in humanity and most the call of
the fallen and the suffering, the call of the self to the self in the
obscure body of the universe. For the awakened individual the
realisation of his truth of being and his inner liberation and
perfection must be his primary seeking, – first, because that is
the call of the Spirit within him, but also because it is only by
liberation and perfection and realisation of the truth of being
that man can arrive at truth of living. A perfected community
also can exist only by the perfection of its individuals, and
perfection can come only by the discovery and affirmation in
life by each of his own spiritual being and the discovery by all of
their spiritual unity and a resultant life unity.   LD, 1050-51

*The present evolutionary crisis comes from a disparity
between the limited faculties of man – mental, ethical and*

spiritual – and the technical and economical means at his disposal.

At present mankind is undergoing an evolutionary crisis in which is concealed a choice of its destiny; for a stage has been reached in which the human mind has achieved in certain directions an enormous development while in others it stands arrested and bewildered and can no longer find its way. A structure of the external life has been raised up by man's ever-active mind and life-will, a structure of an unmanageable hugeness and complexity, for the service of his mental, vital, physical claims and urges, a complex political, social, administrative, economic, cultural machinery, an organised collective means for his intellectual, sensational, aesthetic and material satisfaction. Man has created a system of civilisation which has become too big for his limited mental capacity and understanding and his still more limited spiritual and moral capacity to utilise and manage, a too dangerous servant of his blundering ego[17] and its appetites. For no greater seeing mind, no intuitive soul of knowledge has yet come to his surface of consciousness which could make this basic fullness of life a condition for the free growth of something that exceeded it. This new fullness of the means of life might be, by its power for a release from the incessant unsatisfied stress of his economic and physical needs, an opportunity for the full pursuit of other and greater aims surpassing the material existence, for the discovery of a higher truth and good and beauty, for the discovery of a greater and diviner spirit which would intervene and use life for a higher perfection of the being: but it is being used instead for the multiplication of new wants and an aggressive expansion of the collective ego. At the same time Science has put at his disposal many potencies of the universal Force and has made the life of humanity materially one; but what uses this universal Force is a little human individual or communal ego[17] with nothing universal in its light of knowledge or its movements, no inner sense of power which would create in this physical drawing together of the human world a true life-unity, a mental unity or a spiritual oneness. All that is there is a chaos of clashing mental ideas, urges of individual and collective physical want and need, vital claims and desires, impulses of an ignorant life-push, hungers and calls for life satisfaction of individuals, classes, nations, a rich fungus of political and social and economic nostrums and notions, a hustling medley of slogans and panaceas for which men are ready to oppress and be oppressed, to kill and be killed, to impose them somehow or other by the immense and too formidable means placed at his disposal, in the belief that this is his way out to something ideal. The evolution of human mind and life must necessarily lead towards an increasing universality; but on a basis of ego and segmenting and dividing mind this opening to the universal can only create a vast pullulation of unaccorded ideas and impulses, a surge of enormous powers and desires, a chaotic mass of unassimilated and intermixed mental, vital and physical material of a larger existence which, because it is not taken up by a creative harmonising light of the Spirit, must welter in a universalised confusion and discord out of which it is impossible to build a greater harmonic life.   LD, 1053-54

Without an inner change man can no longer cope with the gigantic development of the outer life.

A life of unity, mutuality and harmony born of a deeper and wider truth of our being is the only truth of life that can successfully replace the imperfect mental constructions of the past which were a combination of association and regulated conflict, an accommodation of egos and interests grouped or dovetailed into each other to form a society, a consolidation by common general life-motives, a unification by need and the pressure of struggle with outside forces. It is such a change and such a reshaping of life for which humanity is blindly beginning to seek, now more and more with a sense that its very existence depends upon finding the way. The evolution of Mind working upon Life has developed an organisation of the activity of Mind and use of Matter which can no longer be supported by human capacity without an inner change. An accommodation of the ego-centric human individuality, separative even in association, to a system of living which demands unity, perfect mutuality, harmony, is imperative. But because the burden which is being laid on mankind is too great for the present littleness of the human personality and its petty mind and small life-instincts, because it cannot operate the needed change, because it is using this new apparatus and organisation to serve the old infra-spiritual and infrarational life-self of humanity, the destiny of the race seems to be heading dangerously, as if impatiently and in spite of itself, under the drive of the vital ego seized by colossal forces which are on the same scale as the huge mechanical organisation of life and scientific knowledge which it has evolved, a scale too large for its reason and will to handle, into a prolonged confusion and perilous crisis and darkness of violent shifting incertitude. Even if this turns out to be a passing phase or appearance and tolerable structural accommodation is found which will enable mankind to proceed less catastrophically on its uncertain journey, this can only be a respite. For the problem is fundamental and in putting it evolutionary Nature in man is confronting herself with a critical choice which must one day be solved in the true sense if the race is to arrive or even to survive. LD, 1055-56

The exaltation of the collectivity, of the State, only substitutes the collective ego for the individual ego.

A rational and scientific formula of the vitalistic and materialistic human being and his life, a search for a perfected economic society and the democratic cultus of the average man are all that the modern mind presents us in this crisis as a light for its solution. Whatever the truth supporting these ideas, this is clearly not enough to meet the need of a humanity which is missioned to evolve beyond itself or, at any rate, if it is to live, must evolve far beyond anything that it at present is. A life-instinct in the race and in the average man himself has felt the inadequacy and has been driving towards a reversal of values or a discovery of new values and a transfer of life to a new foundation. This has taken the form of an attempt to find a simple and ready-made basis of unity, mutuality, harmony for the common life, to enforce it by a suppression of the competitive clash of egos and so to arrive at a life of identity for the community in place of a life of difference. But to realise these desirable ends the means adopted have been the forcible and successful materialisation of a few restricted ideas or slogans enthroned to the exclusion of all other thought, the suppression of the mind of the individual, a mechanised compression of the elements of life, a mechanised unity and drive of the life-force, a coercion of man by the State, the substitution of the communal for the individual ego. The communal ego is idealised as the soul of the nation, the race, the community; but this is a colossal and may turn out to be a fatal error. A forced and imposed unanimity of mind, life, action raised to their highest tension under the drive of something which is thought to be greater, the collective soul, the collective life, is the formula found. But this obscure collective being is not the soul or self of the community; it is a life-force that rises from the subconscient and, if denied the light of guidance by the reason, can be driven only by dark massive forces which are powerful but dangerous for the race because they are alien to the conscious evolution of which man is the trustee and bearer. It is not in this direction that evolutionary Nature has pointed mankind; this is a reversion towards something that she had left behind her.   LD, 1056-57

If humanity is to survive, a radical transformation of human nature is indispensable.

But it has not been found in experience, whatever might have once been hoped, that education and intellectual training by itself can change man; it only provides the human individual and collective ego[17] with better information and a more efficient machinery for its self-affirmation, but leaves it the same unchanged human ego. Nor can human mind and life be cut into perfection, – even into what is thought to be perfection, a constructed substitute, – by any kind of social machinery; matter can be so cut, thought can be so cut, but in our human existence matter and thought are only instruments for the soul and the life-force. Machinery cannot form the soul and life-force into standardised shapes; it can at best coerce them, make soul and mind inert and stationary and regulate the life's outward action; but if this is to be effectively done, coercion and compression of the mind and life are indispensable and that again spells either unprogressive stability or decadence.

There is the possibility that in the swing back from a mechanistic idea of life and society the human mind may seek refuge in a return to the religious idea and a society governed or sanctioned by religion. But organised religion, though it can provide a means of inner uplift for the individual and preserve in it or behind it a way for his opening to spiritual experience, has not changed human life and society; it could not do so because, in governing society, it had to compromise with the lower parts of life and could not insist on the inner change of the whole being; it could insist only on a credal adherence, a formal acceptance of its ethical standards and a conformity to institution, ceremony and ritual. Religion so conceived can give a religio-ethical colour or surface tinge, – sometimes, if it maintains a strong kernel of inner experience, it can generalise to some extent an incomplete spiritual tendency; but it does not transform the race, it cannot create a new principle of the human existence. A total spiritual direction given to the whole life and the whole nature can alone lift humanity beyond itself. Another possible conception akin to the religious solution is the guidance of society by men of spiritual attainment, the brotherhood or unity of all in the faith or in the discipline, the spiritualisation of life and society by the taking up of the old machinery of life into such a unification or inventing a new machinery. This too has been attempted before without success; it was the original founding idea of more than one religion: but the human ego and vital nature were too strong for a religious idea working on the mind and by the mind to overcome its resistance. It is only the full emergence of the soul,[4] the full descent of the native light and power of the Spirit and the consequent replacement or transformation and uplifting of our insufficient mental and vital nature by a spiritual and supra-mental Supernature that can effect this evolutionary miracle.

At first sight this insistence on a radical change of nature might seem to put off all the hope of humanity to a distant evolutionary future; for the transcendence of our normal human nature, a transcendence of our mental, vital and physical being, has the appearance of an endeavour too high and difficult and at present, for man as he is, impossible. Even if it were so, it would still remain the sole possibility for the transmutation of life; for to hope for a true change of human life without a change of human nature is an irrational and unspiritual propo-sition; it is to ask for something unnatural and unreal, an impossible miracle. But what is demanded by this change is not something altogether distant, alien to our existence and radical-ly impossible; for what has to be developed is there in our being and not something outside it: what evolutionary Nature presses for, is an awakening to the knowledge of self, the discovery of Self, the manifestation of the self and spirit within us and the release of its self-knowledge, its self-power, its native self-instrumentation. It is, besides, a step for which the whole of evolution has been a preparation and which is brought closer at each crisis of human destiny when the mental and vital evolu-tion of the being touches a point where intellect and vital force reach some acme of tension and there is a need either for them to collapse, to sink back into a torpor of defeat or a repose of unprogressive quiescence or to rend their way through the veil against which they are straining. What is necessary is that there should be a turn in humanity felt by some or many towards the vision of this change, a feeling of its imperative need, the sense of its possibility, the will to make it possible in themselves and to find the way. That trend is not absent and it must increase with the tension of the crisis in human world-destiny; the need of an escape or a solution, the feeling that there is no other solution than the spiritual cannot but grow and become more imperative under the urgency of critical circumstance. To that call in the being there must always be some answer in the Divine Reality and in Nature.   LD, 1059-60

CHAPTER IV

Standards of Conduct and Spiritual Freedom

Since perfection is progressive, good and evil are shifting quantities and change from time to time their meaning and value.

If we are to be free in the Spirit, if we are to be subject only to the supreme Truth, we must discard the idea that our mental or moral laws are binding on the Infinite or that there can be anything sacrosanct, absolute or eternal even in the highest of our existing standards of conduct. To form higher and higher temporary standards as long as they are needed is to serve the Divine in his world march; to erect rigidly an absolute standard is to attempt the erection of a barrier against the eternal waters in their outflow. Once the nature-bound soul realises this truth, it is delivered from the duality of good and evil. For good is all that helps the individual and the world towards their divine fullness, and evil is all that retards or breaks up that increasing perfection. But since the perfection is progressive, evolutive in Time, good and evil are also shifting quantities and change from time to time their meaning and value. This thing which is evil now and in its present shape must be abandoned was once helpful and necessary to the general and individual progress. That other thing which we now regard as evil may well become in another form and arrangement an element in some future perfection. And on the spiritual level we transcend even this distinction, for we discover the purpose and divine utility of all these things that we call good and evil. Then we have to reject the falsehood in them and all that is distorted, ignorant and obscure in that which is called good no less than in that which is called evil. For we have then to accept only the true and the divine, but to make no other distinction in the eternal processes.

To those who can act only on a rigid standard, to those who

can feel only the human and not the divine values this truth may seem to be a dangerous concession which is likely to destroy the very foundation of morality, confuse all conduct and establish only chaos. Certainly, if the choice must be between an eternal and unchanging ethics and no ethics at all, it would have that result for man in his ignorance. But even on the human level, if we have light enough and flexibility enough to recognise that a standard of conduct may be temporary and yet necessary for its time and to observe it faithfully until it can be replaced by a better, then we suffer no such loss, but lose only the fanaticism of an imperfect and intolerant virtue. In its place we gain openness and a power of continual moral progression, charity, the capacity to enter into an understanding sympathy with all this world of struggling and stumbling creatures and by that charity a better right and a greater strength to help it upon its way. In the end where the human closes and the divine commences, where the mental disappears into the supramental consciousness and the finite precipitates itself into the infinite, all evil disappears into a transcendent divine Good which becomes universal on every plane of consciousness that it touches.

This, then, stands fixed for us that all standards by which we may seek to govern our conduct are only our temporary, imperfect and evolutive attempts to represent to ourselves our stumbling mental progress in the universal self-realisation towards which Nature moves. But the divine manifestation cannot be bound by our little rules and fragile sanctities; for the consciousness behind it is too vast for these things. Once we have grasped this fact, disconcerting enough to the absolutism of our reason, we shall better be able to put in their right place in regard to each other the successive standards that govern the different stages in the growth of the individual and the collective march of mankind. At the most general of them we may cast a passing glance. For we have to see how they stand in relation to that other standardless, spiritual and supramental mode of working for which Yoga[13] seeks and to which it moves by the surrender of the individual to the divine Will and, more

effectively, through his ascent by this surrender to the greater
consciousness in which a certain identity with the dynamic
Eternal becomes possible.   SY, 180-81

*Four main principles successively govern human conduct.
The first two are personal need and the good of the
collectivity.*

There are four main standards of human conduct that make an
ascending scale. The first is personal need, preference and
desire; the second is the law and good of the collectivity; the
third is an ideal ethic; the last is the highest divine law of the
nature.

Man starts on the long career of his evolution with only the
first two of these four to enlighten and lead him; for they
constitute the law of his animal and vital existence, and it is as
the vital and physical animal man that he begins his progress.
The true business of man upon earth is to express in the type of
humanity a growing image of the Divine; whether knowingly or
unknowingly, it is to this end that Nature is working in him
under the thick veil of her inner and outer processes. But the
material or animal man is ignorant of the inner aim of life; he
knows only its needs and its desires and he has necessarily no
other guide to what is required of him than his own perception
of need and his own stirrings and pointings of desire. To satisfy
his physical and vital demands and necessities before all things
else and, in the next rank, whatever emotional or mental
cravings or imaginations or dynamic notions rise in him must be
the first natural rule of his conduct. The sole balancing or
overpowering law that can modify or contradict this pressing
natural claim is the demand put on him by the ideas, needs and
desires of his family, community or tribe, the herd, the pack of
which he is a member.

In itself this seemingly larger and overriding law is no more than
an extension of the vital and animal principle that governs the

individual elementary man; it is the law of the pack or herd. The individual identifies partially his life with the life of a certain number of other individuals with whom he is associated by birth, choice or circumstance. And since the existence of the group is necessary for his own existence and satisfaction, in time, if not from the first, its preservation, the fulfilment of its needs and the satisfaction of its collective notions, desires, habits of living, without which it would not hold together, must come to take a primary place. The satisfaction of personal idea and feeling, need and desire, propensity and habit has to be constantly subordinated, by the necessity of the situation and not from any moral or altruistic motive, to the satisfaction of the ideas and feelings, needs and desires, propensities and habits, not of this or that other individual or number of individuals, but of the society as a whole. This social need is the obscure matrix of morality and of man's ethical impulse.

Man has in him two distinct master impulses, the individualistic and the communal, a personal life and a social life, a personal motive of conduct and a social motive of conduct. The possibility of their opposition and the attempt to find their equation lie at the very roots of human civilisation and persist in other figures when he has passed beyond the vital animal into a highly individualised mental and spiritual progress.

The existence of a social law external to the individual is at different times a considerable advantage and a disadvantage to the development of the divine in man. It is an advantage at first when man is crude and incapable of self-control and self-finding, because it erects a power other than that of his personal egoism through which that egoism may be induced or compelled to moderate its savage demands, to discipline its irrational and often violent movements and even to lose itself sometimes in a larger and less personal egoism. It is a disadvantage to the adult spirit ready to transcend the human formula because it is an external standard which seeks to impose itself on him from outside, and the condition of his perfection is that he shall grow from within and in an increasing freedom, not by the sup-

pression but by the transcendence of his perfected individuality,
not any longer by a law imposed on him that trains and
disciplines his members but by the soul from within breaking
through all previous forms to possess with its light and transmute his members.   SY, 181-84

*A conflict is born of the opposition of the two instinctive
tendencies which govern human action: the individualistic
and the communal.*

In the conflict of the claims of society with the claims of the
individual two ideal and absolute solutions confront one
another. There is the demand of the group that the individual
should subordinate himself more or less completely or even lose
his independent existence in the community, the smaller must
be immolated or self-offered to the larger unit. He must accept
the need of the society as his own need, the desire of the society
as his own desire; he must live not for himself but for the tribe,
clan, commune or nation of which he is a member. The ideal
and absolute solution from the individual's standpoint would be
a society that existed not for itself, for its all-overriding
collective purpose, but for the good of the individual and his
fulfilment, for the greater and more perfect life of all its
members. Representing as far as possible his best self and
helping him to realise it, it would respect the freedom of each of
its members and maintain itself not by law and force but by the
free and spontaneous consent of its constituent persons.

And in the present balance of humanity there is seldom any real
danger of exaggerated individualism breaking up the social
integer. There is continually a danger that the exaggerated
pressure of the social mass by its heavy unenlightened mechanical weight may suppress or unduly discourage the free
development of the individual spirit. For man in the individual
can be more easily enlightened, conscious, open to clear
influences; man in the mass is still obscure, half-conscious,

ruled by universal forces that escape its mastery and its knowledge.   SY, 184-185

> *In order to settle this conflict, a new principle comes in, other and higher than the two conflicting instincts, and aiming both to override and to reconcile them. This third principle is the ethical ideal.*

Above the natural individual law which sets up as our one standard of conduct the satisfaction of our individual needs, preferences and desires and the natural communal law which sets up as a superior standard the satisfaction of the needs, preferences and desires of the community as a whole, there had to arise the notion of an ideal moral law which is not the satisfaction of need and desire, but controls and even coerces or annuls them in the interests of an ideal order that is not animal, not vital and physical, but mental, a creation of the mind's seeking for light and knowledge and right rule and right movement and true order. The moment this notion becomes powerful in man, he begins to escape from the engrossing vital and material into the mental life....

It is therefore essentially an individual standard; it is not a creation of the mass mind. The thinker is the individual; it is he who calls out and throws into forms that which would otherwise remain subconscious in the amorphous human whole. The moral striver is also the individual; self-discipline, not under the yoke of an outer law, but in obedience to an internal light, is essentially an individual effort. But by positing his personal standard as the translation of an absolute moral ideal the thinker imposes it, not on himself alone, but on all the individuals whom his thought can reach and penetrate. And as the mass of individuals come more and more to accept it in idea if only in an imperfect practice or no practice, society also is compelled to obey the new orientation. It absorbs the ideative influence and tries, not with any striking success, to mould its institutions into new forms touched by these higher ideals. But always its instinct is to translate them into binding law, into pattern form, into mechanic custom, into an external social compulsion upon its living units.

For, long after the individual has become partially free, a moral organism capable of conscious growth, aware of an inward life, eager for spiritual progress, society continues to be external in its methods, a material and economic organism, mechanical, more intent upon status and self-preservation than on growth and self-perfection. The greatest present triumph of the thinking and progressive individual over the instinctive and static society has been the power he has acquired by his thought-will to compel it to think also, to open itself to the idea of social justice and righteousness, communal sympathy and mutual compassion, to feel after the rule of reason rather than blind custom as the test of its institutions and to look on the mental and moral assent of its individuals as at least one essential element in the validity of its laws. Ideally at least, to consider light rather than force as its sanction, moral development and not vengeance or restraint as the object even of its penal action, is becoming just possible to the communal mind. The greatest future triumph of the thinker will come when he can persuade the individual integer and the collective whole to rest their life-relation and its union and stability upon a free and harmonious consent and self-adaptation, and shape and govern the external by the internal truth rather than to constrain the inner spirit by the tyranny of the external form and structure.

SY, 186-87

But conflicts do not subside; they seem rather to multiply. Moral laws are arbitrary and rigid; when applied to life, they are obliged to come to terms with it and end in compromises which deprive them of all power.

But even this success that he has gained is rather a thing in potentiality than in actual accomplishment. There is always a disharmony and a discord between the moral law in the individual and the law of his needs and desires, between the moral law proposed to society and the physical and vital needs, desires, customs, prejudices, interests and passions of the caste, the clan, the religious community, the society, the nation. The moralist erects in vain his absolute ethical standard and calls upon all to be faithful to it without regard to consequences.

The first reason is that our moral ideals are themselves for the most part ill-evolved, ignorant and arbitrary, mental constructions rather than transcriptions of the eternal truths of the spirit. Authoritative and dogmatic, they assert certain absolute standards in theory, but in practice every existing system of ethics proves either in application unworkable or is in fact a constant coming short of the absolute standard to which the ideal pretends. If our ethical system is a compromise or a makeshift, it gives at once a principle of justification to the further sterilising compromises which society and the individual hasten to make with it. And if it insists on absolute love, justice, right with an uncompromising insistence, it soars above the head of human possibility and is professed with lip homage but ignored in practice. Even it is found that it ignores other elements in humanity which equally insist on survival but refuse to come within the moral formula. For just as the individual law of desire contains within it invaluable elements of the infinite whole which have to be protected against the tyranny of the absorbing social idea, the innate impulses too both of individual and of collective man contain in them invaluable elements which escape the limits of any ethical formula yet discovered and are yet necessary to the fullness and harmony of an eventual divine perfection.

Moreover, absolute love, absolute justice, absolute right reason in their present application by a bewildered and imperfect humanity come easily to be conflicting principles. Justice often demands what love abhors. Right reason dispassionately considering the facts of nature and human relations in search of a satisfying norm or rule is unable to admit without modification either any reign of absolute justice or any reign of absolute love. And in fact man's absolute justice easily turns out to be in practice a sovereign injustice; for his mind, one-sided and rigid in its constructions, puts forward a one-sided partial and rigorous scheme or figure and claims for it totality and absoluteness and an application that ignores the subtler truth of things and the plasticity of life. All our standards turned into action either waver on a flux of compromises or err by this partiality and unelastic structure. Humanity sways from one orientation to another; the race moves upon a zigzag path led by conflicting claims and, on the whole, works out instinctively what Nature intends, but with much waste and suffering, rather than either what it desires or what it holds to be right or what the highest light from above demands from the embodied spirit.

SY, 187-89

Behind the ethical law which is a false image, a greater truth of a vast consciousness without fetters unveils itself, the supreme law of our divine nature. It determines perfectly our relations with each being and with the totality of the universe, and it also reveals the exact rhythm of the direct expression of the Divine in us. It is the fourth and supreme principle of action which is at the same time imperative law and absolute freedom.

The fact is that when we have reached the cult of absolute ethical qualities and erected the categorical imperative of an ideal law, we have not come to the end of our search or touched the truth that delivers.... And behind the inadequacy of these ethical conceptions something too is concealed that does attach to a supreme Truth; there is here the glimmer of a light and power that are part of a yet unreached divine Nature. But the mental idea of these things is not that light and the moral formulation of them is not that power. These are only representative constructions of the mind that cannot embody the divine spirit which they vainly endeavour to imprison in their cate-

gorical formulas. Beyond the mental and moral being in us is a
greater divine being that is spiritual and supramental; for it is
ony through a large spiritual plane where the mind's formulas
dissolve in a white flame of direct inner experience that we can
reach beyond mind and pass from its constructions to the
vastness and freedom of the supramental realities. There alone
can we touch the harmony of the divine powers that are poorly
mispresented to our mind or framed into a false figure by the
conflicting or wavering elements of the moral law. There alone
the unification of the transformed vital and physical and the
illumined mental man becomes possible in that supramental
spirit which is at once the secret source and goal of our mind
and life and body. There alone is there any possibility of an
absolute justice, love and right – far other than that which we
imagine – at one with each other in the light of a supreme divine
knowledge. There alone can there be a reconciliation of the
conflict between our members.

In other words there is, above society's external law and
man's moral law and beyond them, though feebly and ignorant-
ly aimed at by something within them, a larger truth of a vast
unbound consciousness, a law divine towards which both these
blind and gross formulations are progressive faltering steps that
try to escape from the natural law of the animal to a more
exalted light or universal rule. That divine standard, since the
godhead in us is our spirit moving towards its own concealed
perfection, must be a supreme spiritual law and truth of our
nature. Again, as we are embodied beings in the world with a
common existence and nature and yet individual souls capable
of direct touch with the Transcendent, this supreme truth of
ourselves must have a double character. It must be a law and
truth that discovers the perfect movement, harmony, rhythm of
a great spiritualised collective life and determines perfectly our
relations with each being and all beings in Nature's varied
oneness. It must be at the same time a law and truth that
discovers to us at each moment the rhythm and exact steps of
the direct expression of the Divine in the soul, mind, life, body
of the individual creature. And we find in experience that this

supreme light and force of action in its highest expression is at once an imperative law and an absolute freedom. It is an imperative law because it governs by immutable Truth our every inner and outer movement. And yet at each moment and in each movement the absolute freedom of the Supreme handles the perfect plasticity of our conscious and liberated nature.

SY, 189-91

CHAPTER V

The Development of the Spiritual Man

Spirituality is something else than intellectuality; its appearance is the sign that a Power greater than mind is striving to emerge in its turn.

It is quite true that to a surface view Life seems only an operation of Matter, Mind an activity of Life, and it might seem to follow that what we call the soul or spirit is only a power of mentality, soul a fine form of mind, spirituality a high activity of the embodied mental being. But this is a superficial view of things due to the thought's concentrating on the appearance and process and not looking at what lies behind the process. One might as well on the same lines have concluded that electricity is only a product or operation of water and cloud matter, because it is in such a field that lightning emerges; but a deeper inquiry has shown that both cloud and water have, on the contrary, the energy of electricity as their foundation, their constituent power or energy-substance: that which seems to be a result is, – in its reality, though not in its form, – the origin; the effect is in the essence pre-existent to the apparent cause, the principle of the emergent activity precedent to its present field of action. So it is throughout evolutionary Nature; Matter could not have become animate if the principle of Life had not been there constituting Matter and emerging as a phenomenon of Life-in-Matter; Life-in-Matter could not have begun to feel, perceive, think, reason, if the principle of Mind had not been there behind life and substance, constituting it as its field of operation and emergent in the phenomenon of a thinking life and body: so too spirituality emerging in Mind is the sign of a power which itself has founded and constituted life, mind and body and is now emerging as a spiritual being in a living and thinking body. How far this emergence will go, whether it will become dominant and transform its instrument, is a subsequent question; but what is necessary first to posit is the existence of Spirit as something else than Mind and greater than Mind, spirituality as something other than mentality and the spiritual being therefore as something distinct from the mental being: Spirit is a final evolutionary emergence because it is the original involutionary element and factor. Evolution is an inverse action of the involution[3]: what is an ultimate and last derivation in the involution is the first to appear in the evolution; what was original and primal in the involution is in the evolution the last and supreme emergence.   LD, 852-53

> *Spirituality is a progressive awakening to the inner reality of our being, to a spirit, self, soul which is other than our mind, life and body. It is an inner aspiration to know, to enter into contact and union with the greater Reality beyond, which also pervades the universe and dwells in us, and, as a result of that aspiration, that contact and that union, a turning, a conversion, a birth into a new being.*

In the animal mind is not quite distinct from its own life-matrix and life-matter; its movements are so involved in the life-movements that it cannot detach itself from them, cannot stand separate and observe them; but in man mind has become separate, he can become aware of his mental operations as distinct from his life-operations, his thought and will can disengage themselves from his sensations and impulses, desires and emotional reactions, can become detached from them, observe and control them, sanction or cancel their functioning: he does not as yet know the secrets of his being well enough to be aware of himself decisively and with certitude as a mental being in a life and body, but he has that impression and can take inwardly that position. So too at first soul in man does not appear as something quite distinct from mind and from mentalised life; its movements are involved in the mind-movements, its operations seem to be mental and emotional activities; the mental human being is not aware of a soul in him standing back from the mind and life and body, detaching itself, seeing and controlling and moulding their action and formation but, as the inner evolution proceeds, this is precisely what can, must and does happen, – it is the long-delayed but inevitable next step in our evolutionary destiny. There can be a decisive emergence in which the being separates itself from thought and sees itself in an inner silence as the spirit in mind, or separates itself from the life movements, desires, sensations, kinetic impulses and is aware of itself as the spirit supporting life, or separates itself from the body sense and knows itself as a spirit ensouling Matter: this is the discovery of ourselves as the Purusha,[8] a mental being or a life-soul or a subtle self supporting the body. This is taken by many as a sufficient discovery of the true self and in a certain sense they are right; for it is the Self or Spirit that so represents itself in regard to the activities of Nature, and this revelation of its presence is enough to disengage the spiritual element: but self-discovery can go farther, it can even put aside all relation to form or action of Nature. For it is seen that these selves are representations of a divine Entity to which mind, life and body are only forms and instruments: we are then the Soul looking at Nature, knowing all her dynamisms in us, not by mental perception and observation, but by an intrinsic consciousness and its direct sense of things and its intimate exact vision, able therefore by its emergence to put a close control on our nature and change it. When there is a complete silence in the being, either a stillness of the whole being or a stillness behind unaffected by surface movements, then we can become aware of a Self, a spiritual substance of our being, an existence exceeding even the soul-individuality, spreading itself into universality, surpassing all dependence on any natural form or action, extending itself upward into a transcendence of which the limits are not visible. It is these liberations of the spiritual part in us which are the decisive steps of the spiritual evolution in Nature.

When there is the decisive emergence, one sign of it is the status

or action in us of an inherent, intrinsic, self-existent consciousness which knows itself by the mere fact of being, knows all that
is in itself in the same way by identity with it, begins even to see
all that to our mind seems external in the same manner, by a
movement of identity or by an intrinsic direct consciousness
which envelops, penetrates, enters into its object, discovers
itself in the object, is aware in it of something that is not mind or
life or body. There is, then, evidently a spiritual consciousness
which is other than the mental, and it testifies to the existence of
a spiritual being in us which is other than our surface mental
personality. But at first this consciousness may confine itself to a
status of being separate from the action of our ignorant surface
nature, observing it, limiting itself to knowledge, to a seeing of
things with a spiritual sense and vision of existence. For action it
may still depend upon the mental, vital, bodily instruments, or it
may allow them to act according to their own nature and itself
remain satisfied with self-experience and self-knowledge, with
an inner liberation, an eventual freedom: but it may also and
usually does exercise a certain authority, governance, influence
on thought, life movement, physical action, a purifying uplifting
control compelling them to move in a higher and purer truth of
themselves, to obey or be an instrumentation of an influx of
some diviner Power or a luminous direction which is not mental
but spiritual and can be recognised as having a certain divine
character, – the inspiration of a greater Self or the command of
the Ruler of all being, the Ishwara.[18] Or the nature may obey the
psychic entity's intimations, move in an inner light, follow an
inner guidance. This is already a considerable evolution and
amounts to a beginning at least of a psychic and spiritual
transformation. But it is possible to go farther; for the spiritual
being, once inwardly liberated, can develop in mind the higher
states of being that are its own natural atmosphere and bring
down a supramental energy and action which are proper to the
Truth-consciousness; the ordinary mental instrumentation, life-
instrumentation, physical instrumentation even, could then be
entirely transformed and become parts no longer of an ignorance however much illumined, but of a supramental creation

which would be the true action of a spiritual truth-consciousness and knowledge.

. . . it must therefore be emphasised that spirituality is not a high
intellectuality, not idealism, not an ethical turn of mind or moral
purity and austerity, not religiosity or an ardent and exalted
emotional fervour, not even a compound of all these excellent
things; a mental belief, creed or faith, an emotional aspiration, a
regulation of conduct according to a religious or ethical formula
are not spiritual achievement and experience. These things are
of considerable value to mind and life; they are of value to the
spiritual evolution itself as preparatory movements disciplining,
purifying or giving a suitable form to the nature; but they still
belong to the mental evolution, – the beginning of a spiritual
realisation, experience, change is not yet there. Spirituality is in
its essence an awakening to the inner reality of our being, to a
spirit, self, soul which is other than our mind, life and body, an
inner aspiration to know, to feel, to be that, to enter into contact
with the greater Reality beyond and pervading the universe
which inhabits also our own being, to be in communion with It
and union with It, and a turning, a conversion, a transformation
of our whole being as a result of the aspiration, the contact, the
union, a growth or waking into a new becoming or new being, a
new self, a new nature.   LD, 853-57

*In her attempt to open up the inner being, Nature has
followed four main lines – religion, occultism, spiritual
thought and an inner spiritual realisation and experience.*

There are four main lines which Nature has followed in her
attempt to open up the inner being, – religion, occultism,
spiritual thought and an inner spiritual realisation and experience: the three first are approaches, the last is the decisive
avenue of entry. All these four powers have worked by a
simultaneous action, more or less connected, sometimes in a
variable collaboration, sometimes in dispute with each other,

sometimes in a separate independence. Religion has admitted an occult element in its ritual, ceremony, sacraments; it has leaned upon spiritual thinking, deriving from it sometimes a creed or theology, sometimes its supporting spiritual philosophy, – the former, ordinarily, is the occidental method, the latter the oriental: but spiritual experience is the final aim and achievement of religion, its sky and summit.

... each of these means or approaches corresponds to something in our total being and therefore to something necessary to the total aim of her evolution. There are four necessities of man's self-expansion if he is not to remain this being of the surface ignorance seeking obscurely after the truth of things and collecting and systematising fragments and sections of knowledge, the small limited and half-competent creature of the cosmic Force which he now is in his phenomenal nature. He must know himself and discover and utilise all his potentialities: but to know himself and the world completely he must go behind his own and its exterior, he must dive deep below his own mental surface and the physical surface of Nature. This he can only do by knowing his inner mental, vital, physical and psychic being[6] and its powers and movements and the universal laws and processes of the occult Mind and Life which stand behind the material front of the universe: that is the field of occultism, if we take the word in its widest significance. He must know also the hidden Power or Powers that control the world: if there is a Cosmic Self or Spirit or a Creator, he must be able to enter into relation with It or Him and be able to remain in whatever contact or communion is possible, get into some kind of tune with the master Beings of the universe or with the universal Being and its universal will or a supreme Being and His supreme will, follow the law It gives him and the assigned or revealed aim of his life and conduct, raise himself towards the highest height that It demands of him in his life now or in his existence hereafter; if there is no such universal or supreme Spirit or Being, he must know what there is and how to lift himself to it out of his present imperfection and impotence.

This approach is the aim of religion: its purpose is to link the human with the Divine and in so doing sublimate the thought and life and flesh so that they may admit the rule of the soul and spirit. But this knowledge must be something more than a creed or a mystic revelation; his thinking mind must be able to accept it, to correlate it with the principle of things and the observed truth of the universe: this is the work of philosophy, and in the field of the truth of the spirit it can only be done by a spiritual philosophy, whether intellectual in its method or intuitive. But all knowledge and endeavour can reach its fruition only if it is turned into experience and has become a part of the consciousness and its established operations; in the spiritual field all this religious, occult or philosophical knowledge and endeavour must, to bear fruition, end in an opening up of the spiritual consciousness, in experiences that found and continually heighten, expand and enrich that consciousness and in the building of a life and action that is in conformity with the truth of the spirit: this is the work of spiritual realisation and experience.   LD, 860, 861-62

Only spiritual realisation and experience can achieve the change of the mental being into a spiritual being.

But none of these three lines of approach can by themselves entirely fulfil the greater and ulterior intention of Nature; they cannot create in mental man the spiritual being, unless and until they open the door to spiritual experience. It is only by an inner realisation of what these approaches are seeking after, by an overwhelming experience or·by many experiences building up an inner change, by a transmutation of the consciousness, by a liberation of the spirit from its present veil of mind, life and body that there can emerge the spiritual being. That is the final line of the soul's progress towards which the others are pointing and, when it is ready to disengage itself from the preliminary approaches, then the real work has begun and the turning-point of the change is no longer distant. Till then all that the human mental being has reached is a familiarity with the idea of things beyond him, with the possibility of an other-worldly movement, with the ideal of some ethical perfection; he may have made too some contact with greater Powers or Realities which help his mind or heart or life. A change there may be, but not the transmutation of the mental into the spiritual being. Religion and its thought and ethics and occult mysticism in ancient times produced the priest and the mage, the man of piety, the just man, the man of wisdom, many high points of mental manhood; but it is only after spiritual experience through the heart and mind began that we see arise the saint, the prophet, the Rishi,[13] the Yogi, the seer, the spiritual sage and the mystic, and it is the religions in which these types of spiritual manhood came into being that have endured, covered the globe and given mankind all its spiritual aspiration and culture.

The last or highest emergence is the liberated man who has realised the Self and Spirit within him, entered into the cosmic consciousness, passed into union with the Eternal and, so far as he still accepts life and action, acts by the light and energy of the Power within him working through his human instruments of Nature. The largest formulation of this spiritual change and achievement is a total liberation of soul, mind, heart and action, a casting of them all into the sense of the cosmic Self and the Divine Reality. The spiritual evolution of the individual has then found its way and thrown up its range of Himalayan eminences and its peaks of highest nature. Beyond this height and largeness there opens only the supramental ascent or the incommunicable Transcendence. LD, 880-81, 882

Mysticism and spirituality have been criticised from two points of view. These criticisms should be examined before proceeding further:

1. The mystic turns away from life.

... the mystic in this view is the man who turns aside into the unreal, into occult regions of a self-constructed land of chimeras and loses his way there.... The mystic either detaches himself from life as the other-worldly ascetic or the aloof visionary and therefore cannot help life, or else he brings no better solution or result than the practical man or the man of intellect and reason....

[To this kind of criticism one can reply that the true task of spirituality] is not to solve human problems on the past or present mental basis, but to create a new foundation of our being and our life and knowledge. The ascetic or other-worldly tendency of the mystic is an extreme affirmation of his refusal to accept the limitations imposed by material Nature: for his very reason of being is to go beyond her; if he cannot transform her, he must leave her. At the same time the spiritual man has not stood back altogether from the life of humanity; for the sense of unity with all beings, the stress of a universal love and compassion, the will to spend the energies for the good of all creatures,* are central to the dynamic outflowering of the spirit: he has turned therefore to help, he has guided as did the ancient Rishis or the prophets, or stooped to create and, where he has done so with something of the direct power of the Spirit, the results have been prodigious. But the solution of the problem which spirituality offers is not a solution by external means, though these also have to be used, but by an inner change, a transformation of the consciousness and nature.

If no decisive but only a contributory result, an accretion of some new finer elements to the sum of the consciousness, has been the general consequence and there has been no life-transformation, it is because man in the mass has always deflected the spiritual impulsion, recanted from the spiritual ideal or held it only as a form and rejected the inward change. Spirituality cannot be called upon to deal with life by a non-spiritual method or attempt to cure its ills by the panaceas, the political, social or other mechanical remedies which the mind is constantly attempting and which have always failed and will continue to fail to solve anything. The most drastic changes made by these means change nothing; for the old ills exist in a new form: the aspect of the outward environment is altered, but man remains what he was; he is still an ignorant mental being misusing or not effectively using his knowledge, moved by ego and governed by vital desires and passions and the needs of the body, unspiritual and superficial in his outlook, ignorant of his own self and the forces that drive and use him. His life-constructions have a value as expressions of his individual and collective being in the stage to which they have reached or as a machinery for the convenience and welfare of his vital and physical parts and a field and medium for his mental growth, but they cannot take him beyond his present self or serve as a machinery to transform him; his and their perfection can only come by his farther evolution. Only a spiritual change, an evolution of his being from the superficial mental towards the deeper spiritual consciousness, can make a real and effective difference. To discover the spiritual being in himself is the main business of the spiritual man and to help others towards the same evolution is his real service to the race; till that is done, an outward help can succour and alleviate, but nothing or very little more is possible.

It is true that the spiritual tendency has been to look more beyond life than towards life. It is true also that the spiritual change has been individual and not collective; its result has been successful in the man, but unsuccessful or only indirectly operative in the human mass. The spiritual evolution of Nature is still in process and incomplete, – one might almost say, still only beginning, – and its main preoccupation has been to affirm and develop a basis of spiritual consciousness and knowledge and to create more and more a foundation or formation for the vision of that which is eternal in the truth of the spirit.

2. *Mystical knowledge is purely subjective.*

Another objection to the mystic and his knowledge is urged, not against its effect upon life but against his method of the discovery of Truth and against the Truth that he discovers. . . . But it is urged that the actual result of this method is not one truth common to all, there are great differences; the conclusion suggested is that this knowledge is not truth at all but a subjective mental formation. But this objection is based on a misunderstanding of the nature of spiritual knowledge. Spiritual truth is a truth of the spirit, not a truth of the intellect, not a mathematical theorem or a logical formula. It is a truth of the Infinite, one in an infinite diversity, and it can assume an infinite variety of aspects and formations: in the spiritual evolution it is inevitable that there should be a many-sided passage and reaching to the one Truth, a many-sided seizing of it; this many-sidedness is the sign of the approach of the soul to a living reality, not to an abstraction or a constructed figure of things that can be petrified into a dead or stony formula. The hard logical and intellectual notion of truth as a single idea which all must accept, one idea or system of ideas defeating all other ideas or systems, or a single limited fact or single formula of facts which all must recognise, is an illegitimate transference from the limited truth of the physical field to the much more complex and plastic field of life and mind and spirit.

This transference has been responsible for much harm; it brings into thought narrowness, limitation, an intolerance of the necessary variation and multiplicity of view-points without which there can be no totality of truth-finding, and by the narrowness and limitation much obstinacy in error. It reduces philosophy to an endless maze of sterile disputes; religion has been invaded by this misprision and infected with credal dogmatism, bigotry and intolerance. The truth of the spirit is a truth of being and consciousness and not a truth of thought: mental ideas can only represent or formulate some facet, some mind-translated principle or power of it or enumerate its aspects, but to know it one has to grow into it and be it; without the growing and being there can be no true spiritual knowledge. The fundamental truth of spiritual experience is one, its consciousness is one, everywhere it follows the same general lines and tendencies of awakening and growth into spiritual being; for these are the imperatives of the spiritual consciousness. But also there are, based on those imperatives, numberless possibilities of variation of experience and expression: the centralisation and harmonisation of these possibles, but also the intensive sole following out of any line of experience are both of them necessary movements of the emerging spiritual Conscious-Force within us. Moreover, the accommodation of mind and life to the spiritual truth, its expression in them, must vary with the mentality of the seeker so long as he has not risen above all need of such accommodation or such limiting expression. It is this mental and vital element which has created the oppositions that still divide spiritual seekers or enter into their differing affirmations of the truth that they experience. This difference and variation is needed for the freedom of spiritual search and spiritual growth: to overpass differences is quite possible, but that is most easily done in pure experience; in mental formulation the difference must remain until one can exceed mind altogether and in a highest consciousness integralise, unify and harmonise the many-sided truth of the Spirit.

...the supreme Self is one, but the souls of the Self are many and as is the soul's formation of nature, so will be its spiritual self-expression. A diversity in oneness is the law of the manifestation; the supramental unification and integration must harmonise these diversities, but to abolish them is not the intention of the Spirit in Nature.   LD, 883-88

CHAPTER VI

The Triple Transformation

If the final goal of terrestrial evolution were only to awaken man to the supreme Reality and to release him from ignorance and bondage, so that the liberated soul could find elsewhere a higher state of being or merge into this Reality, *the task would be accomplished with the advent of the spiritual man. But there is also in us an aspiration for the mastery of Nature and her transformation, for a greater perfection in the earthly existence itself.*

If it is the sole intention of Nature in the evolution of the spiritual man to awaken him to the supreme Reality and release him from herself, or from the Ignorance in which she as the Power of the Eternal has masked herself, by a departure into a higher status of being elsewhere, if this step in the evolution is a close and an exit, then in the essence her work has been already accomplished and there is nothing more to be done. The ways have been built, the capacity to follow them has been developed, the goal or last height of the creation is manifest; all that is left is for each soul to reach individually the right stage and turn of its development, enter into the spiritual ways and pass by its own chosen path out of this inferior existence. But we have supposed that there is a farther intention, – not only a revelation of the Spirit, but a radical and integral transformation of Nature. There is a will in her to effectuate a true manifestation of the embodied life of the Spirit, to complete what she has begun by a passage from the Ignorance to the Knowledge, to throw off her mask and to reveal herself as the luminous Consciousness-Force [18] carrying in her the eternal Existence and its universal Delight of being. It then becomes obvious that there is something not yet accomplished, there becomes clear to view the much that has still to be done, *bhūri aspaṣṭa kartvam*;

there is a height still to be reached, a wideness still to be covered by the eye of vision, the wing of the will, the self-affirmation of the Spirit in the material universe. What the evolutionary Power has done is to make a few individuals aware of their souls, conscious of their selves, aware of the eternal being that they are, to put them into communion with the Divinity or the reality which is concealed by her appearances: a certain change of nature prepares, accompanies or follows upon this illumination, but it is not the complete and radical change which establishes a secure and settled new principle, a new creation, a permanent new order of being in the field of terrestrial Nature. The spiritual man has evolved, but not the supramental being who shall thenceforward be the leader of that Nature.   LD, 889-90

To be established permanently, this new order of existence demands a radical change of the entire human nature. In this transformation, there are three phases.

It must become the normal nature of a new type of being; as mind is established here on a basis of Ignorance seeking for Knowledge and growing into Knowledge, so supermind must be established here on a basis of Knowledge growing into its own greater Light. But this cannot be so long as the spiritual-mental being has not risen fully to supermind and brought down its powers into terrestrial existence. For the gulf between Mind and Supermind has to be bridged, the closed passages opened and roads of ascent and descent created where there is now a void and a silence.... There must first be the psychic change, the conversion of our whole present nature into a soul-instrumentation; on that or along with that there must be the spiritual change, the descent of a higher Light, Knowledge, Power, Force, Bliss, Purity into the whole being, even into the lowest recesses of the life and body, even into the darkness of our subconscience; last, there must supervene the supramental transmutation, – there must take place as the crowning movement the ascent into the supermind and the transforming descent of the supramental Consciousness into our entire being and nature.   LD, 890-91

> *The first phase of this transformation can be called psychic: the soul, or psychic being, has to come forward and take the lead of the whole being.*

At the beginning the soul in Nature, the psychic[4] entity, whose unfolding is the first step towards a spiritual change, is an entirely veiled part of us, although it is that by which we exist and persist as individual beings in Nature. The other parts of our natural composition are not only mutable but perishable; but the psychic entity in us persists and is fundamentally the same always: it contains all essential possibilities of our manifestation but is not constituted by them; it is not limited by what it manifests, not contained by the incomplete forms of the manifestation, not tarnished by the imperfections and impurities, the defects and deprivations of the surface being. It is an ever-pure flame of the divinity in things and nothing that comes to it, nothing that enters into our experience can pollute its purity or extinguish the flame. This spiritual stuff is immaculate and luminous and, because it is perfectly luminous, it is immediately, intimately, directly aware of truth of being and truth of nature; it is deeply conscious of truth and good and beauty because truth and good and beauty are akin to its own native character, forms of something that is inherent in its own substance. It is aware also of all that contradicts these things, of all that deviates from its own native character, of falsehood and evil and the ugly and the unseemly; but it does not become these things nor is it touched or changed by these opposites of itself which so powerfully affect its outer instrumentation of mind, life and body. For the soul, the permanent being in us, puts forth and uses mind, life and body as its instruments, undergoes the envelopment of their conditions, but it is other and greater than its members.

If the psychic entity had been from the beginning unveiled and known to its ministers, not a secluded King in a screened chamber, the human evolution would have been a rapid soul-outflowering, not the difficult, chequered and disfigured development it now is; but the veil is thick and we know not the secret Light within us, the light in the hidden crypt of the heart's innermost sanctuary. Intimations rise to our surface from the psyche, but our mind does not detect their source; it takes them for its own activities because, before even they come to the surface, they are clothed in mental substance: thus ignorant of their authority, it follows or does not follow them according to its bent or turn at the moment. If the mind obeys the urge of the vital ego, then there is little chance of the psychic at all controlling the nature or manifesting in us something of its secret spiritual stuff and native movement; or, if the mind is over-confident to act in its own smaller light, attached to its own judgment, will and action of knowledge, then also the soul will remain veiled and quiescent and wait for the mind's farther evolution. For the psychic part within is there to support the natural evolution, and the first natural evolution must be the development of body, life and mind, successively, and these must act each in its own kind or together in their ill-assorted partnership in order to grow and have experience and evolve. The soul gathers the essence of all our mental, vital and bodily experience and assimilates it for the farther evolution of our existence in Nature; but this action is occult and not obtruded on the surface. In the early material and vital stages of the evolution of being there is indeed no consciousness of soul; there are psychic activities, but the instrumentation, the form of these activities are vital and physical, – or mental when the mind is active. For even the mind, so long as it is primitive or is developed but still too external, does not recognise their deeper character.

Man is in his self a unique Person, but he is also in his manifestation of self a multiperson; he will never succeed in being master of himself until the Person imposes itself on his multipersonality and governs it: but this can only be imperfectly done by the surface mental will and reason; it can be perfectly done only if he goes within and finds whatever central being is by its predominant influence at the head of all his expression and action. In inmost truth it is his soul that is this central being, but in outer fact it is often one or other of the part beings in him that rules, and this representative of the soul, this deputy self he can mistake for the inmost soul principle.   LD, 891-92, 897-98

> *In the course of evolution, the soul, in order to emerge successfully and turn the being towards the supreme Reality, uses three dynamic images of this supreme Reality: Truth, Beauty and Good. Three ways thus open before the seeker.*

A first condition of the soul's complete emergence is a direct contact in the surface being with the spiritual Reality. Because it comes from that, the psychic element in us turns always towards whatever in phenomenal Nature seems to belong to a higher Reality and can be accepted as its sign and character. At first, it seeks this Reality through the good, the true, the beautiful, through all that is pure and fine and high and noble: but although this touch through outer signs and characters can modify and prepare the nature, it cannot entirely or most inwardly and profoundly change it. For such an inmost change the direct contact with the Reality itself is indispensable since nothing else can so deeply touch the foundations of our being and stir it or cast the nature by its stir into a ferment of transmutation. Mental representations, emotional and dynamic figures have their use and value; Truth, Good and Beauty are in themselves primary and potent figures of the Reality, and even in their forms as seen by the mind, as felt by the heart, as realised in the life can be lines of an ascent: but it is in a spiritual substance and being of them and of itself that That which they represent has to come into our experience.   LD, 900-01

1. The way of the intellect or of knowledge.

The soul may attempt to achieve this contact mainly through the thinking mind as intermediary and instrument; it puts a psychic impression on the intellect and the larger mind of insight and intuitional intelligence and turns them in that direction. At its highest the thinking mind is drawn always towards the impersonal; in its search it becomes conscious of a spiritual essence, an impersonal Reality which expresses itself in all these outward signs and characters but is more than any formation or manifesting figure. It feels something of which it becomes intimately and invisibly aware, – a supreme Truth, a supreme Beauty, a supreme Purity, a supreme Bliss; it bears the increasing touch, less and less impalpable and abstract, more and more spiritually real and concrete, the touch and pressure of an Eternity and Infinity which is all this that is and more. There is a pressure from this Impersonality that seeks to mould the whole mind into a form of itself; at the same time the impersonal secret and law of things becomes more and more visible. The mind develops into the mind of the sage, at first the high mental thinker, then the spiritual sage who has gone beyond the abstractions of thought to the beginnings of a direct experience. As a result the mind becomes pure, large, tranquil, impersonal; there is a similar tranquillising influence on the parts of life: but otherwise the result may remain incomplete; for the mental change leads more naturally towards an inner status and an outer quietude, but, poised in this purifying quietism, not drawn like the vital parts towards a discovery of new life-energies, does not press for a full dynamic effect on the nature.

A higher endeavour through the mind does not change this balance; for the tendency of the spiritualised mind is to go on upwards and, since above itself the mind loses its hold on forms, it is into a vast formless and featureless impersonality that it enters. It becomes aware of the unchanging Self, the sheer Spirit, the pure bareness of an essential Existence, the formless Infinite and the nameless Absolute. This culmination can be arrived at more directly by tending immediately beyond all forms and figures, beyond all ideas of good or evil or true or false or beautiful or unbeautiful to That which exceeds all dualities, to the experience of a supreme oneness, infinity, eternity or other ineffable sublimation of the mind's ultimate and extreme percept of Self or Spirit. A spiritualised consciousness is achieved and the life falls quiet, the body ceases to need and to clamour, the soul itself merges into the spiritual silence. But this transformation through the mind does not give us the integral transformation; the psychic transmutation is replaced by a spiritual change on the rare and high summits, but this is not the complete divine dynamisation of Nature.

LD, 901-02

2. The way of the heart or of emotion.

A second approach made by the soul to the direct contact is through the heart: this is its own more close and rapid way because its occult seat is there, just behind in the heart-centre, in close contact with the emotional being in us; it is consequently through the emotions that it can act best at the beginning with its native power, with its living force of concrete experience. It is through a love and adoration of the All-beautiful and All-blissful, the All-Good, the True, the spiritual Reality of love, that the approach is made; the aesthetic and emotional parts join together to offer the soul, the life, the whole nature to that which they worship. This approach through adoration can get its full power and impetus only when the mind goes beyond impersonality to the awareness of a supreme Personal Being: then all becomes intense, vivid, concrete; the heart's emotion, feeling, spiritualised sense reach their absolute; an entire self-giving becomes possible, imperative. The nascent spiritual man makes his appearance in the emotional nature as the devotee, the bhakta;[16] if, in addition, he becomes directly aware of his soul and its dictates, unites his emotional with his psychic personality and changes his life and vital parts by purity, God-ecstasy, the love of God and men and all creatures into a thing of spiritual beauty, full of divine light and good, he develops into the saint and reaches the highest inner experience and most considerable change of nature proper to this way of approach to the Divine Being. But for the purpose of an integral transformation this too is not enough; there must be a transmutation of the thinking mind and all the vital and physical parts of consciousness in their own character.

LD, 902-03

3. The way of the will or of action.

This larger change can be partly attained by adding to the experiences of the heart a consecration of the pragmatic will which must succeed in carrying with it – for otherwise it cannot be effective, – the adhesion of the dynamic vital part which supports the mental dynamis and is our first instrument of outer action. This consecration of the will in works proceeds by a gradual elimination of the ego-will and its motive-power of desire; the ego subjects itself to some higher law and finally effaces itself, seems not to exist or exists only to serve a higher Power or a higher Truth or to offer its will and acts to the Divine Being as an instrument. The law of being and action or the light of Truth which then guides the seeker, may be a clarity or power or principle which he perceives on the highest height of which his mind is capable; or it may be a truth of the divine Will which he feels present and working within him or guiding him by a Light or a Voice or a Force or a Divine Person or Presence. In the end by this way one arrives at a consciousness in which one feels the Force or Presence acting within and moving or governing all the actions and the personal will is entirely surrendered or identified with that greater Truth-Will, Truth-Power or Truth-Presence.

LD, 903

These three ways, combined and followed concurrently, have a most powerful effect.

A combination of all these three approaches, the approach of the mind, the approach of the will, the approach of the heart, creates a spiritual or psychic condition of the surface being and nature in which there is a larger and more complex openness to the psychic light within us and to the spiritual Self or the Ishwara,[18] to the Reality now felt above and enveloping and penetrating us. In the nature there is a more powerful and many-sided change, a spiritual building and self-creation, the appearance of a composite perfection of the saint, the selfless worker and the man of spiritual knowledge.   LD, 903-04

A shifting of the consciousness, a withdrawal within, becomes imperative at this stage, in order to reach the central being, the true Soul, and to allow it to become the guide and sovereign of the nature.

But, for this change to arrive at its widest totality and profound completeness, the consciousness has to shift its centre and its static and dynamic position from the surface to the inner being; it is there that we must find the foundation for our thought, life and action. For to stand outside on our surface and to receive from the inner being and follow its intimations is not a sufficient transformation; one must cease to be the surface personality and become the inner Person, the Purusha. . . . It then becomes possible to pass through to the depths of our being and from the depths so reached a new consciousness can be formed, both behind the exterior self and in it, joining the depths to the surface. There must grow up within us or there must manifest a consciousness more and more open to the deeper and the higher being, more and more laid bare to the cosmic Self and Power and to what comes down from the Transcendence, turned to a higher Peace, permeable to a greater light, force and ecstasy, a consciousness that exceeds the small personality and surpasses the limited light and experience of the surface mind, the limited force and aspiration of the normal life-conscious-ness, the obscure and limited responsiveness of the body.

For this penetration into the luminous crypt of the soul one has to get through all the intervening vital stuff to the psychic centre within us, however long, tedious or difficult may be the process. The method of detachment from the insistence of all mental and vital and physical claims and calls and impulsions, a concentration in the heart, austerity, self-purification and rejection of the old mind-movements and life-movements, rejection of the ego of desire, rejection of false needs and false habits, are all useful aids to this difficult passage: but the strongest, most central way is to found all such or other methods on a self-offering and surrender of ourselves and of our parts of nature to the Divine Being, the Ishwara. A strict obedience to the wise and intuitive leading of a Guide is also normal and necessary for all but a few specially gifted seekers.   LD, 904-05, 907

Two principal results follow this emergence: first an effective guidance and mastery which unmask and reject all that is false and obscure or all that opposes the divine realisation; then, a spontaneous influx of spiritual experiences of all kinds.

As the crust of the outer nature cracks, as the walls of inner separation break down, the inner light gets through, the inner fire burns in the heart, the substance of the nature and the stuff of consciousness refine to a greater subtlety and purity, and the deeper psychic experiences, those which are not solely of an inner mental or inner vital character, become possible in this subtler, purer, finer substance; the soul begins to unveil itself, the psychic personality reaches its full stature. The soul, the psychic entity, then manifests itself as the central being which upholds mind and life and body and supports all the other powers and functions of the Spirit; it takes up its greater function as the guide and ruler of the nature. A guidance, a governance begins from within which exposes every movement to the light of Truth, repels what is false, obscure, opposed to the divine realisation: every region of the being, every nook and

corner of it, every movement, formation, direction, inclination
of thought, will, emotion, sensation, action, reaction, motive,
disposition, propensity, desire, habit of the conscious or subconscious physical, even the most concealed, camouflaged,
mute, recondite, is lighted up with the unerring psychic light,
their confusions dissipated, their tangles disentangled, their
obscurities, deceptions, self-deceptions precisely indicated and
removed; all is purified, set right, the whole nature harmonised,
modulated in the psychic key, put in spiritual order.

This is the first result, but the second is a free inflow of all kinds
of spiritual experience, experience of the Self, experience of
the Ishwara and the Divine Shakti,[18] experience of cosmic consciousness, a direct touch with cosmic forces and with the
occult movements of universal Nature, a psychic sympathy and
unity and inner communication and interchanges of all kinds
with other beings and with Nature, illuminations of the mind by
knowledge, illuminations of the heart by love and devotion and
spiritual joy and ecstasy, illuminations of the sense and the body
by higher experience, illuminations of dynamic action in the
truth and largeness of a purified mind and heart and soul, the
certitudes of the divine light and guidance, the joy and power of
the divine force working in the will and the conduct. These
experiences are the result of an opening outward of the inner
and inmost being and nature; for then there comes into play the
soul's power of unerring inherent consciousness, its vision, its
touch on things which is superior to any mental cognition; there
is there, native to the psychic consciousness in its pure working,
an immediate sense of the world and its beings, a direct inner
contact with them and a direct contact with the Self and with
the Divine, – a direct knowledge, a direct sight of Truth and of
all truths, a direct penetrating spiritual emotion and feeling, a
direct intuition of right will and right action, a power to rule
and to create an order of the being not by the gropings of the
superficial self, but from within, from the inner truth of self and
things and the occult realities of Nature.　　LD, 907-909

The second phase of the transformation may be called spiritual; it is an opening to an Infinity above us, an eternal Presence, a boundless Self, an infinite Existence, an infinity of Consciousness, an infinity of Bliss, an All-Power.

But all this change and all this experience, though psychic and spiritual in essence and character, would still be, in its parts of life-effectuation, on the mental, vital and physical level.... A highest spiritual transformation must intervene on the psychic or psycho-spiritual change; the psychic movement inward to the inner being, the Self or Divinity within us, must be completed by an opening upward to a supreme spiritual status or a higher existence. This can be done by our opening into what is above us, by an ascent of consciousness into the ranges of overmind[20] and supramental nature in which the sense of Self and Spirit is ever unveiled and permanent and in which the self-luminous instrumentation of the Self and Spirit is not restricted or divided as in our mind-nature, life-nature, body-nature. This also the psychic change makes possible; for as it opens us to the cosmic consciousness now hidden from us by many walls of limiting individuality, so also it opens us to what is now superconscient to our normality because it is hidden from us by the strong, hard and bright lid of mind, – mind constricting, dividing and separative. The lid thins, is slit, breaks asunder or opens and disappears under the pressure of the psycho-spiritual change and the natural urge of the new spiritualised consciousness towards that of which it is an expression here.

If the rift in the lid of mind is made, what happens is an opening of vision to something above us or a rising up towards it or a descent of its powers into our being. What we see by the opening of vision is an Infinity above us, an eternal Presence or an infinite Existence, an infinity of consciousness, an infinity of bliss, – a boundless Self, a boundless Light, a boundless Power, a boundless Ecstasy. It may be that for a long time all that is obtained is the occasional or frequent or constant vision of it and a longing and aspiration, but without anything further, because, although something in the mind, heart or other part of the being has opened to this experience, the lower nature as a whole is too heavy and obscure as yet for more. But there may be, instead of this first wide awareness from below or subsequently to it, an ascension of the mind to heights above: the nature of the heights we may not know or clearly discern, but some consequence of the ascent is felt; there is often too an awareness of infinite ascension and return but no record or translation of that higher state.   LD, 909-910, 911

The spiritual change culminates in a permanent ascension from the lower consciousness to the higher consciousness, followed by an effective permanent descent of the higher nature into the lower.

In time the ascent comes to be made at will and the consciousness brings back and retains some effect or some gain of its temporary sojourn in these higher countries of the Spirit. These ascents take place for many in trance, but are perfectly possible in a concentration of the waking consciousness or, where that consciousness has become sufficiently psychic, at any unconcentrated moment by an upward attraction or affinity. But these two types of contact with the superconscient, though they can be powerfully illuminating, ecstatic or liberating, are by themselves insufficiently effective: for the full spiritual transformation more is needed, a permanent ascension from the lower into the higher consciousness and an effectual permanent descent of the higher into the lower nature.   LD, 912

A new consciousness begins to form with new forces of thought and sight, and a power of direct spiritual realisation which is more than thought or sight.

This experience of descent can take place as a result of the other two movements or automatically before either has happened, through a sudden rift in the lid or a percolation, a downpour or an influx. A light descends and touches or envelops or penetrates the lower being, the mind, the life or the body; or a presence or a power or a stream of knowledge pours in waves or currents, or there is a flood of bliss or a sudden ecstasy; the contact with the superconscient has been established. For such experiences repeat themselves till they become normal, familiar and well-understood, revelatory of their contents and their significance which may have at first been involved and wrapped into secrecy by the figure of the covering experience. For a knowledge from above begins to descend, frequently, constantly, then uninterruptedly, and to manifest in the mind's quietude or silence; intuitions and inspirations, revelations born of a greater sight, a higher truth and wisdom, enter into the being, a luminous intuitive discrimination works which dispels all darkness of understanding or dazzling confusions, puts all in order; a new consciousness begins to form, the mind of a high wide self-existent thinking knowledge or an illumined or an intuitive or an overmental consciousness with new forces of thought or sight and a greater power of direct spiritual realisation which is more than thought or sight, a greater becoming in the spiritual substance of our present being; the heart and the sense become subtle, intense, large to embrace all existence, to see God, to feel and hear and touch the Eternal, to make a deeper and a closer unity of self and the world in a transcendent realisation. Other decisive experiences, other changes of consciousness determine themselves which are corollaries and consequences of this fundamental change. No limit can be fixed to this revolution; for it is in its nature an invasion by the Infinite.

For this new consciousness has itself the nature of infinity: it brings to us the abiding spiritual sense and awareness of the Infinite and Eternal with a great largeness of the nature and a breaking down of its limitations; immortality becomes no longer a belief or an experience but a normal self-awareness; the close presence of the Divine Being, his rule of the world and of our

self and natural members, his force working in us and everywhere, the peace of the infinite, the joy of the infinite are now
concrete and constant in the being; in all sights and forms one
sees the Eternal, the Reality, in all sounds one hears it, in all
touches feels it; there is nothing else but its forms and
personalities and manifestations; the joy or adoration of the
heart, the embrace of all existence, the unity of the spirit are
abiding realities. The consciousness of the mental creature is
turning or has been already turned wholly into the consciousness of the spiritual being. This is the second of the three
transformations; uniting the manifested existence with what is
above it, it is the middle step of the three, the decisive transition
of the spiritually evolving nature.   LD, 912-14

> *To make this new creation permanent and perfect, the very*
> *foundation of our nature of ignorance must be transfigured*
> *and a greater power, a supramental Force must intervene to*
> *accomplish that transfiguration. This is the third phase: the*
> *supramental transformation.*

As the psychic change has to call in the spiritual to complete it,
so the first spiritual change has to call in the supramental
transformation to complete it. For all these steps forward are,
like those before them, transitional; the whole radical change in
the evolution from a basis of Ignorance to a basis of Knowledge
can only come by the intervention of the supramental Power
and its direct action in earth-existence.

This then must be the nature of the third and final transformation which finishes the passage of the soul through the
Ignorance and bases its consciousness, its life, its power and
form of manifestation on a complete and completely effective
self-knowledge. The Truth-Consciousness, finding evolutionary
Nature ready, has to descend into her and enable her to liberate
the supramental principle within her; so must be created the
supramental and spiritual being as the first unveiled manifestation of the truth of the Self and Spirit in the material universe.

                                                    LD, 917-18

CHAPTER VII

The Ascent Towards Supermind

It is difficult to conceive intellectually what the Supermind is; and to describe it, another language would be needed than the poor abstract counters of the mind.

The psychic transformation and the first stages of the spiritual transformation are well within our conception; their perfection would be the perfection, wholeness, consummated unity of a knowledge and experience which is already part of things realised, though only by a small number of human beings. But the supramental change in its process carries us into less explored regions; it initiates a vision of heights of consciousness which have indeed been glimpsed and visited, but have yet to be discovered and mapped in their completeness. The highest of these peaks or elevated plateaus of consciousness, the supramental, lies far beyond the possibility of any satisfying mental scheme or map of it or any grasp of mental seeing and description. It would be difficult for the normal unillumined or untransformed mental conception to express or enter into something that is based on so different a consciousness with a radically different awareness of things; even if they were seen or conceived by some enlightenment or opening of vision, another language than the poor abstract counters used by our mind would be needed to translate them into terms by which their reality could become at all seizable by us. As the summits of human mind are beyond animal perception, so the movements of supermind are beyond the ordinary human mental conception: it is only when we have already had experience of a higher intermediate consciousness that any terms attempting to describe supramental being could convey a true meaning to our intelligence; for then, having experienced something akin to what is described, we could translate an inadequate language into a figure of what we knew. If the mind cannot enter into the

nature of supermind, it can look towards it through these high
and luminous approaches and catch some reflected impression
of the Truth, the Right, the Vast which is the native kingdom of
the free Spirit.   LD, 919-20

> *The transition from mind to Supermind is a passage from
> Nature into Supernature. For that very reason it cannot be
> achieved by a mere effort of our mind or our unaided
> aspiration. Overmind and Supermind are involved and
> hidden in the earth-nature; but, in order that they may
> emerge in us, there is needed a pressure of the same powers
> already formulated in their full natural force on their own
> superconscient planes. The powers of the Superconscience
> must descend into us and uplift us and transform our being.*

The transition to Supermind through Overmind is a passage
from Nature as we know it into Super-Nature.[8] It is by that very
fact impossible for any effort of the mere Mind to achieve; our
unaided personal aspiration and endeavour cannot reach it: our
effort belongs to the inferior power of Nature; a power of the
Ignorance cannot achieve by its own strength or characteristic
or available methods what is beyond its own domain of nature.
All the previous ascensions have been effectuated by a secret
Consciousness-Force[2] operating first in Inconscience and then
in the Ignorance: it has worked by an emergence of its involved
powers to the surface, powers concealed behind the veil and
superior to the past formulations of Nature, but even so there is
needed a pressure of the same superior powers already formulated in their full natural force on their own planes; these
superior planes create their own foundation in our subliminal[6]
parts and from there are able to influence the evolutionary
process on the surface. Overmind and Supermind are also
involved and occult in earth-Nature, but they have no formations on the accessible levels of our subliminal inner consciousness; there is as yet no overmind being or organised overmind
nature, no supramental being or organised supermind nature

acting either on our surface or in our normal subliminal parts:
for these greater powers of consciousness are superconscient to
the level of our ignorance. In order that the involved principles·
of Overmind and Supermind should emerge from their veiled
secrecy, the being and powers of the superconscience must
descend into us and uplift us and formulate themselves in our
being and powers; this descent is a *sine qua non* of the transition
and transformation.

For a real transformation there must be a direct and unveiled
intervention from above; there would be necessary too a total
submission and surrender of the lower consciousness, a cessation of its insistence, a will in it for its separate law of action to
be completely annulled by transformation and lose all rights
over our being. If these two conditions can be achieved even
now by a conscious call and will in the spirit and a participation
of our whole manifested and inner being in its change and
elevation, the evolution, the transformation can take place by a
comparatively swift conscious change; the supramental Consciousness-Force from above and the evolving Consciousness-
Force from behind the veil acting on the awakened awareness
and will of the mental human being would accomplish by their
united power the momentous transition. There would be no
farther need of a slow evolution counting many millenniums for
each step, the halting and difficult evolution operated by Nature
in the past in the unconscious creatures of the Ignorance.

LD, 921, 922

*What should be the preparation for the supramental trans-
formation? First, an increasing control of the individual over
his own natures and a more and more conscious participation in the action of the Supernature.*

It is a first condition of this change that the mental Man we now
are should become inwardly aware and in possession of his own
deeper law of being and its processes; he must become the

psychic and inner mental being, master of his energies, no longer a slave of the movements of the lower Prakriti,[8] in control of it, seated securely in a free harmony with a higher law of Nature.... In human mind there is the first appearance of an observing intelligence that regards what is being done and of a will and choice that have become conscious; but the consciousness is still limited and superficial: the knowledge also is limited and imperfect, it is a partial intelligence, a half understanding, groping and empirical in great part or, if rational, then rational by constructions, theories, formulas. There is not as yet a luminous seeing which knows things by a direct grasp and arranges them with a spontaneous precision according to the seeing, according to the scheme of their inherent truth; although there is a certain element of instinct and intuition and insight which has some beginning of this power, the normal character of human intelligence is an inquiring reason or reflective thought which observes, supposes, infers, concludes, arrives by labour at a constructed truth, a constructed scheme of knowledge, a deliberately arranged action of its own making.

It is only a free and entire intuitive consciousness which would be able to see and to grasp things by direct contact and penetrating vision or a spontaneous truth-sense born of an underlying unity or identity and arrange an action of Nature according to the truth of Nature. This would be a real participation by the individual in the working of the universal Consciousness-Force; the individual Purusha[8] would become the master of his own executive energy and at the same time a conscious partner, agent, instrument of the Cosmic Spirit in the working of the universal Energy: the universal Energy would work through him, but he also would work through her and the harmony of the intuitive truth would make this double working a single action. A growing conscious participation of this higher and more intimate kind must be one accompaniment of the transition from our present state of being to a state of supernature.

Thus the individuality would become more and more powerful and effective in proportion as it realised itself as a centre and formation of the universal and transcendent Being and Nature. For as the progression of the change proceeded, the energy of the liberated individual would be no longer the limited energy of mind, life and body, with which it started; the being would emerge into and put on, – even as there would emerge in him and descend into him, assuming him into it, – a greater light of Consciousness and a greater action of Force: his natural existence would be the instrumentation of a superior Power, an overmental and supramental Consciousness-Force, the power of the original Divine Shakti.[18] All the processes of the evolution would be felt as the action of a supreme and universal Consciousness, a supreme and universal Force working in whatever way it chose, on whatever level, within whatever self-determined limits, a conscious working of the transcendent and cosmic Being, the action of the omnipotent and omniscient World-Mother raising the being into herself, into her super-nature. In place of the Nature of Ignorance with the individual as its closed field and unconscious or half-conscious instrument, there would be a Supernature of the divine Gnosis[9] and the individual soul would be its conscious, open and free field and instrument, a participant in its action, aware of its purpose and process, aware too of its own greater Self, the universal, the transcendent Reality, and of its own Person as illimitably one with that and yet an individual being of Its being, an instrument and a spiritual centre.

A first opening towards this participation in an action of Supernature is a condition of the turn towards the last, the supramental transformation: for this transformation is the completion of a passage from the obscure harmony of a blind automatism with which Nature sets out to the luminous authentic spontaneity, the infallible motion of the self-existent truth of the Spirit. The evolution begins with the automatism of Matter and of a lower life in which all obeys implicitly the drive of Nature, fulfils mechanically its law of being and therefore succeeds in maintaining a harmony of its limited type of

existence and action; it proceeds through the pregnant confusion of the mind and life of a humanity driven by this inferior
Nature but struggling to escape from her limitations, to master
and drive and use her; it emerges into a greater spontaneous
harmony and automative self-fulfilling action founded on the
spiritual Truth of things. In this higher state the consciousness
will see that Truth and follow the line of its energies with a full
knowledge, with a strong participation and instrumental
mastery, a complete delight in action and existence. There will
be a luminous and enjoyed perfection of unity with all instead of
a blind and suffered subjection of the individual to the
universal, and at every moment the action of the universal in the
individual and the individual in the universal will be enlightened and governed by the rule of the transcendent Supernature.

LD, 922-24, 927-28

*A second condition consists in a conscious obedience, a
surrender of our whole being to the light, the truth and force
from above.*

But this highest condition is difficult and must evidently take
long to bring about; for the participation and consent of the
Purusha to the transition is not sufficient; there must be also the
consent and participation of the Prakriti. It is not only the
central thought and will that have to acquiesce, but all the parts
of our being must assent and surrender to the law of the
spiritual Truth; all has to learn to obey the government of the
conscious Divine Power in the members. There are obstinate
difficulties in our being, born of its evolutionary constitution,
which militate against this assent. For some of these parts are
still subject to the inconscience and subconscience and to the
lower automatism of habit or so-called law of the nature, –
mechanical habit of mind, habit of life, habit of instinct, habit of
personality, habit of character, the ingrained mental, vital,
physical needs, impulses, desires of the natural man, the old
functionings of all kinds that are rooted there so deep that it

would seem as if we had to dig to abysmal foundations in order to get them out ... at each step of the transition the assent of the Purusha is needed and there must be too the consent of each part of the nature to the action of the higher power for its change. There must be then a conscious self-direction of the mental being in us towards this change, this substitution of Supernature for the old nature, this transcendence. The rule of conscious obedience to the higher truth of the spirit, the surrender of the whole being to the light and power that come from the Supernature, is a second condition which has to be accomplished slowly and with difficulty by the being itself before the supramental transformation can become at all possible.

It follows that the psychic and the spiritual transformation must be far advanced, even as complete as may be, before there can be any beginning of the third and consummating supramental change; for it is only by this double transmutation that the self-will of the Ignorance can be totally altered into a spiritual obedience to the remoulding truth and will of the greater Consciousness of the Infinite. A long, difficult stage of constant effort, energism, austerity of the personal will, *tapasya*,[12] has ordinarily to be traversed before a more decisive stage can be reached in which a state of self-giving of all the being to the Supreme Being and the Supreme Nature can become total and absolute. LD, 929

A third condition is the unification of the whole being around the true self and the opening of the individual to the cosmic consciousness.

A unification of the entire being by a breaking down of the wall between the inner and outer nature, – a shifting of the position and centration of the consciousness from the outer to the inner self, a firm foundation on this new basis, a habitual action from this inner self and its will and vision and an opening up of the individual into the cosmic consciousness, – is another necessary condition for the supramental change. It would be chimerical to hope that the supreme Truth-consciousness[9] can establish itself in the narrow formulation of our surface mind and heart and life, however turned towards spirituality. All the inner centres[27] must have burst open and released into action their capacities; the psychic[4] entity must be unveiled and in control. If this first change establishing the being in the inner and larger, a Yogic in place of an ordinary consciousness has not been done, the greater transmutation is impossible. Moreover the individual must have sufficiently universalised himself, he must have recast his individual mind in the boundlessness of a cosmic mentality, enlarged and vivified his individual life into the immediate sense and direct experience of the dynamic motion of the universal life, opened up the communications of his body with the forces of universal Nature, before he can be capable of a change which transcends the present cosmic formulation and lifts him beyond the lower hemisphere of universality into a consciousness belonging to its spiritual upper hemisphere. Besides he must have already become aware of what is now to him super-conscient; he must be already a being conscious of the higher spiritual Light, Power, Knowledge, Ananda,[2] penetrated by its descending influences, new-made by a spiritual change.

The spiritual evolution obeys the logic of a successive unfolding; it can take a new decisive main step only when the previous main step has been sufficiently conquered: even if certain minor stages can be swallowed up or leaped over by a rapid and brusque ascension, the consciousness has to turn back to assure itself that the ground passed over is securely annexed to the new condition. It is true that the conquest of the Spirit supposes the execution in one life or a few lives of a process that in the ordinary course of Nature would involve a slow and uncertain procedure of centuries or even of millenniums: but this is a question of the speed with which the steps are traversed; a greater or concentrated speed does not eliminate the steps themselves or the necessity of their successive surmounting. The increased rapidity is possible only because the conscious participation of the inner being is there and the power of the Supernature is already at work in the half-transformed lower nature, so that the steps which would otherwise have had to be taken tentatively in the night of Inconscience or Ignorance can now be taken in an increasing light and power of Knowledge.

LD, 930-32

Four steps of ascent lead from the human intelligence to the Supermind; these are:

1. Higher Mind

Our first decisive step out of our human intelligence, our normal mentality, is an ascent into a higher Mind, a mind no longer of mingled light and obscurity or half-light, but a large clarity of the spirit. Its basic substance is a unitarian sense of being with a powerful multiple dynamisation capable of the formation of a multitude of aspects of knowledge, ways of action, forms and significances of becoming, of all of which there is a spontaneous inherent knowledge.... It is a luminous thought-mind, a mind of Spirit-born conceptual knowledge. An all-awareness emerging from the original identity, carrying the truths the identity held in itself, conceiving swiftly, victoriously, multitudinously, formulating and by self-power of the Idea effectually realising its conceptions, is the character of this greater mind of knowledge.

But here in this greater Thought there is no need of a seeking and self-critical ratiocination, no logical motion step by step towards a conclusion, no mechanism of express or implied deductions and inferences, no building or deliberate concatenation of idea with idea in order to arrive at an ordered sum or outcome of knowledge....

This higher consciousness is a Knowledge formulating itself on a basis of self-existent all-awareness and manifesting some part of its integrality, a harmony of its significances put into thought-form. It can freely express itself in single ideas, but its most characteristic movement is a mass ideation, a system or totality of truth-seeing at a single view; the relations of idea with idea, of truth with truth are not established by logic but pre-exist and emerge already self-seen in the integral whole. There is an initiation into forms of an ever-present but till now inactive knowledge, not a system of conclusions from premises or data; this thought is a self-revelation of eternal Wisdom, not an acquired knowledge.

This is the Higher Mind in its aspect of cognition; but there is also the aspect of will, of dynamic effectuation of the Truth: here we find that this greater more brilliant Mind works always on the rest of the being, the mental will, the heart and its feelings, the life, the body, through the power of thought, through the idea-force. It seeks to purify through knowledge, to deliver through knowledge, to create by the innate power of knowledge. The idea is put into the heart or the life as a force to be accepted and worked out; the heart and life become conscious of the idea and respond to its dynamisms and their substance begins to modify itself in that sense, so that the feelings and actions become the vibrations of this higher wisdom, are informed with it, filled with the emotion and the sense of it: the will and the life impulses are similarly charged with its power and its urge of self-effectuation; even in the body the idea works so that, for example, the potent thought and will of health replaces its faith in illness and its consent to illness, or the idea* of strength calls in the substance, power, motion, vibration of strength; the idea generates the force and form proper to the idea and imposes it on our substance of Mind, Life or Matter. It is in this way that the first working proceeds; it charges the whole being with a new and superior consciousness, lays a foundation of change, prepares it for a superior truth of existence.   LD, 939-41

2. *Illumined Mind*

This greater Force is that of the Illumined Mind, a Mind no longer of higher Thought, but of spiritual light. Here the clarity of the spiritual intelligence, its tranquil daylight, gives place or subordinates itself to an intense lustre, a splendour and illumination of the spirit: a play of lightnings of spiritual truth and power breaks from above into the consciousness and adds to the calm and wide enlightenment and the vast descent of peace which characterise or accompany the action of the larger conceptual-spiritual principle, a fiery ardour of realisation and a rapturous ecstasy of knowledge. A downpour of inwardly visible Light very usually envelops this action; for it must be noted that, contrary to our ordinary conceptions, light is not primarily a material creation and the sense or vision of light accompanying the inner illumination is not merely a subjective visual image or a symbolic phenomenon: light is primarily a spiritual manifestation of the Divine Reality illuminative and creative; material light is a subsequent representation or conversion of it into Matter for the purposes of the material Energy. There is also in this descent the arrival of a greater dynamic, a golden drive, a luminous 'enthousiasmos' of inner force and power which replaces the comparatively slow and deliberate process of the Higher Mind by a swift, sometimes a vehement, almost a violent impetus of rapid transformation.

The Illumined Mind does not work primarily by thought, but by vision; thought is here only a subordinate movement expressive of sight. The human mind, which relies mainly on thought, conceives that to be the highest or the main process of knowledge, but in the spiritual order thought is a secondary and not indispensable process.

A consciousness that proceeds by sight, the consciousness of the seer, is a greater power for knowledge than the consciousness of the thinker. The perceptual power of the inner sight is greater and more direct than the perceptual power of thought: it is a spiritual sense that seizes something of the substance of Truth and not only her figure; but it outlines the figure also and at the same time catches the significance of the figure, and it can embody her with a finer and bolder revealing outline and a larger comprehension and power of totality than thought-conception can manage.   LD, 944-46

3. Intuitive Mind

But these two stages of the ascent enjoy their authority and can get their own united completeness only by a reference to a third level; for it is from the higher summits where dwells the intuitional being that they derive the knowledge which they turn into thought or sight and bring down to us for the mind's transmutation. Intuition is a power of consciousness nearer and more intimate to the original knowledge by identity; for it is always something that leaps out direct from a concealed identity.... This close perception is more than sight, more than conception: it is the result of a penetrating and revealing touch which carries in it sight and conception as part of itself or as its natural consequence. A concealed or slumbering identity, not yet recovering itself, still remembers or conveys by the intuition its own contents and the intimacy of its self-feeling and self-vision of things, its light of truth, its overwhelming and automatic certitude.

In the human mind the intuition is even such a truth-remembrance or truth-conveyance, or such a revealing flash or blaze breaking into a great mass of ignorance or through a veil of nescience: but we have seen that it is subject there to an invading mixture or a mental coating or an interception and substitution; there is too a manifold possibility of misinterpretation which comes in the way of the purity and fullness of its action. Moreover, there are seeming intuitions on all levels of the being which are communications rather than intuitions, and these have a very various provenance, value and character. The infrarational "mystic", so styled, – for to be a true mystic it is not sufficient to reject reason and rely on sources of thought or action of which one has no understanding, – is often inspired by such communications on the vital level from a dark and dangerous source. In these circumstances we are driven to rely mainly on the reason and are disposed even to control the suggestions of the intuition – or the pseudo-intuition, which is the more frequent phenomenon, – by the observing and discriminating intelligence; for we feel in our intellectual part that we cannot be sure otherwise what is the true thing and what the mixed or adulterated article or false substitute. But this largely discounts for us the utility of the intuition: for the reason is not in this field a reliable arbiter, since its methods are different, tentative, uncertain, an intellectual seeking; even though it itself really relies on a camouflaged intuition for its conclusions, – for without that help it could not choose its course or arrive at any assured finding, – it hides this dependence from itself under the process of a reasoned conclusion or a verified conjecture. An intuition passed in judicial review by the reason ceases to be an intuition and can only have the authority of the reason for which there is no inner source of direct certitude. But even if the mind became predominantly an intuitive mind reliant upon its portion of the higher faculty, the co-ordination of its cognitions and its separated activities, – for in mind these would always be apt to appear as a series of imperfectly connected flashes, – would remain difficult so long as this new mentality has not a conscious liaison with its suprarational source or a self-uplifting access to a higher plane of consciousness in which an intuitive action is pure and native.

Intuition is always an edge or ray or outleap of a superior light; it is in us a projecting blade, edge or point of a far-off supermind light entering into and modified by some intermediate truth-mind substance above us and, so modified, again entering into and very much blinded by our ordinary or ignorant mind-substance; but on that higher level to which it is native its light is unmixed and therefore entirely and purely veridical, and its rays are not separated but connected or massed together in a play of waves of what might almost be called in the Sanskrit poetic figure a sea or mass of "stable lightnings". When this original or native Intuition begins to descend into us in answer to an ascension of our consciousness to its level or as a result of our finding of a clear way of communication with it, it may continue to come as a play of lightning-flashes, isolated or in constant action; but at this stage the judgment of reason becomes quite inapplicable, it can only act as an observer or registrar understanding or recording the more luminous intimations, judgments and discriminations of the higher power. To complete or verify an isolated intuition or discriminate its nature, its application, its limitations, the receiving consciousness must rely on another completing intuition or be able to call down a massed intuition capable of putting all in place. For once the process of the change has begun, a complete transmutation of the stuff and activities of the mind into the substance, form and power of intuition is imperative; until then, so long as the process of consciousness depends upon the lower intelligence serving or helping out or using the intuition, the result can only be a survival of the mixed Knowledge-Ignorance uplifted or relieved by a higher light and force acting in its parts of Knowledge.

Intuition has a fourfold power. A power of revelatory truth-seeing, a power of inspiration or truth-hearing, a power of truth-touch or immediate seizing of significance, which is akin to the ordinary nature of its intervention in our mental intelligence, a power of true and automatic discrimination of the orderly and exact relation of truth to truth, – these are the fourfold potencies of Intuition. Intuition can therefore perform all the action of reason, – including the function of logical intelligence, which is to work out the right relation of things and the right relation of idea, – but by its own superior process and with steps that do not fail or falter.   LD, 946-49

4. Overmind

The next step of the ascent brings us to the Overmind; the intuitional change can only be an introduction to this higher spiritual overture. But we have seen that the Overmind, even when it is selective and not total in its action, is still a power of cosmic consciousness, a principle of global knowledge which carries in it a delegated light from the supramental Gnosis.[9] It is, therefore, only by an opening into the cosmic consciousness that the overmind ascent and descent can be made wholly possible: a high and intense individual opening upwards is not sufficient, – to that vertical ascent towards summit Light there must be added a vast horizontal expansion of the consciousness into some totality of the Spirit.... When the overmind descends, the predominance of the centralising ego-sense is entirely subordinated, lost in largeness of being and finally abolished; a wide cosmic perception and feeling of a boundless universal self and movement replaces it: many motions that were formally ego-centric may still continue, but they occur as' currents or ripples in the cosmic wideness. Thought, for the most part, no longer seems to originate individually in the body or the person but manifests from above or comes in upon the cosmic mind-waves: all inner individual sight or intelligence of things is now a revelation or illumination of what is seen or comprehended, but the source of the revelation is not in one's separate self but in the universal knowledge; the feelings, emotions, sensations are similarly felt as waves from the same cosmic immensity breaking upon the subtle and the gross body and responded to in kind by the individual centre of the universality; for the body is only a small support or even less, a point of relation, for the action of a vast cosmic instrumentation. In this boundless largeness, not only the separate ego but all sense of individuality, even of a subordinated or instrumental individuality, may entirely disappear; the cosmic existence, the cosmic consciousness, the cosmic delight, the play of cosmic forces are alone left: if the delight or the centre of Force is felt in what was the personal mind, life or body, it is not with a sense of personality but as a field of manifestation, and this sense of the delight or of the action of Force is not confined to the person or the body but can be felt at all points in an unlimited consciousness of unity which pervades everywhere.

But there can be many formulations of overmind consciousness and experience; for the Overmind has a great plasticity and
is a field of multiple possibilities. In place of an uncentred and
unplaced diffusion there may be the sense of the universe in
oneself or as oneself: but there too this self is not the ego; it is an
extension of a free and pure essential self-consciousness or it is
an identification with the All, – the extension or the identification constituting a cosmic being, a universal individual.... In the
transition towards the Supermind this centralising action tends
towards the discovery of a true individual replacing the dead
ego, a being who is in his essence one with the supreme Self, one
with the universe in extension and yet a cosmic centre and
circumference of the specialised action of the Infinite.

The overmind change is the final consummating movement of
the dynamic spiritual transformation; it is the highest possible
status-dynamis of the Spirit in the spiritual-mind plane. It takes
up all that is in the three steps below it and raises their
characteristic workings to their highest and largest power,
adding to them a universal wideness of consciousness and force,
a harmonious concert of knowledge, a more manifold delight of
being. But there are certain reasons arising from its own
characteristic status and power that prevent it from being the
final possibility of the spiritual evolution. It is a power, though
the highest power, of the lower hemisphere;[20] although its basis
is a cosmic unity, its action is an action of division and
interaction, an action taking its stand on the play of the
multiplicity. Its play is, like that of all Mind, a play of
possibilities; although it acts not in the Ignorance but with the
knowledge of the truth of these possibilities, yet it works them
out through their own independent evolution of their powers.

LD, 950-53

*The Overmind descent is not sufficient to transform wholly
the Inconscience; the Supramental Force alone is capable of
achieving this.*

In the terrestrial evolution itself the overmind descent would not be able to transform wholly the Inconscience; all that it would do would be to transform in each man it touched the whole conscious beings, inner and outer, personal and universally impersonal, into its own stuff and impose that upon the Ignorance illumining it into cosmic truth and knowledge. But a basis of Nescience would remain; it would be as if a sun and its system were to shine out in an original darkness of Space and illumine everything as far as its rays could reach so that all that dwelt in the light would feel as if no darkness were there at all in their experience of existence. But outside that sphere or expanse of experience the original darkness would still be there and, since all things are possible in an overmind structure, could reinvade the island of light created within its empire.... Also by this much evolution there could be no security against the downward pull of gravitation of the Inconscience which dissolves all the formations that life and mind build in it, swallows all things that arise out of it or are imposed upon it and disintegrates them into their original matter. The liberation from this pull of the Inconscience and a secured basis for a continuous divine or gnostic evolution would only be achieved by a descent of the Supermind into the terrestrial formula, bringing into it the supreme law and light and dynamis of the Spirit and penetrating with it and transforming the inconscience of the material basis. A last transition from Overmind to Supermind and a descent of Supermind must therefore intervene at this stage of evolutionary Nature.

A transformation of human nature can only be achieved when the substance of the being is so steeped in the spiritual principle that all its movements are a spontaneous dynamism and a harmonised process of the Spirit. But even when the higher powers and their intensities enter into the substance of the Inconscience, they are met by this blind opposing Necessity and are subjected to this circumscribing and diminishing law of the nescient substance. It opposes them with its strong titles of an established and inexorable Law, meets always the claim of life with the law of death, the demand of Light with the need of a relief of shadow and a background of darkness, the sovereignty and freedom and dynamism of the Spirit with its own force of adjustment by limitation, demarcation by incapacity, foundation of energy on the repose of an original Inertia. There is an occult truth behind its negations which only the Supermind with its reconciliation of contraries in the original Reality can take up and so discover the pragmatic solution of the enigma. Only the supramental Force can entirely overcome this difficulty of the fundamental Nescience; for with it enters an opposite and luminous imperative Necessity which underlies all things and is the original and final self-determining truth-force of the self-existent· Infinite. This greater luminous spiritual Necessity and its sovereign imperative alone can displace or entirely penetrate, transform into itself and so replace the blind Ananke of the Inconscience.   LD, 953-54, 961-62

CHAPTER VIII

The Gnostic Being

The difficulty in understanding and describing the supra-mental nature comes from the fact that in its very essence, it is consciousness and power of the Infinite.

As we reach in our thought the line at which the evolution of Mind into Overmind passes over into an evolution of Overmind into Supermind, we are faced with a difficulty which amounts almost to an impossibility. For we are moved to seek for some precise idea, some clear mental description of the supramental or gnostic existence of which evolutionary Nature in the Ignorance is in travail; but by crossing this extreme line of sublimated Mind the consciousness passes out of the sphere, exceeds the characteristic action and escapes from the grasp, of mental perception and knowledge.... Our normal perception or imagination or formulation of things spiritual and things mundane is mental, but in the gnostic change the evolution crosses a line beyond which there is a supreme and radical reversal of consciousness and the standards and forms of mental cognition are no longer sufficient: it is difficult for mental thought to understand or describe supramental nature.

Mental nature and mental thought are based on a conscious-ness of the finite; supramental nature is in its very grain a consciousness and power of the Infinite. Supramental Nature sees everything from the stand-point of oneness and regards all things, even the greatest multiplicity and diversity, even what are to the mind the strongest contradictions, in the light of that oneness; its will, ideas, feelings, sense are made of the stuff of oneness, its actions proceed upon that basis. Mental nature, on the contrary, thinks, sees, wills, feels, senses with division as a starting-point and has only a constructed understanding of unity; even when it experiences oneness, it has to act from the oneness on a basis of limitation and difference. But the supramental, the divine life is a life of essential, spontaneous and inherent unity. It is impossible for the mind to forecast in detail what the supramental change must be in its parts of life action and outward behaviour or lay down for it what forms it shall create for the individual or the collective existence. LD, 964-65

One can, however, describe in a general way the passage from the Overmind to the Supermind and form an idea of the supramental existence in its initial step.

This passage is the stage at which the supermind gnosis[9] can take over the lead of the evolution from the overmind and build the first foundations of its own characteristic manifestation and unveiled activities; it must be marked therefore by a decisive but long-prepared transition from an evolution in the Ignorance to an always progressive evolution in the Knowledge. It will not be a sudden revelation and effectuation of the absolute Supermind and the supramental being as they are in their own plane, the swift apocalypse of a truth-conscious existence ever self-fulfilled and complete in self-knowledge; it will be the phenomenon of the supramental being descending into a world of evolutionary becoming and forming itself there, unfolding the powers of the gnosis within the terrestrial nature.

[This revelation] can assume the formula of a truth-conscious existence founded in an inherent self-knowledge but at the same time taking up into itself mental nature and the nature of life and material body. For the supermind as the truth conscious-ness of the Infinite has in its dynamic principle the infinite power of a free self-determination. It can hold all knowledge in itself and yet put forward in formulation only what is needed at each stage of an evolution; it formulates whatever is in accor-dance with the Divine Will in manifestation and the truth of the thing to be manifested. It is by this power that it is able to hold back its knowledge, hide its own character and law of action and manifest Overmind and under Overmind a world of ignorance in which the being wills on its surface not to know and even puts itself under the control of a pervading Nescience. But in this new stage the veil thus put on will be lifted....

LD, 966-67

The supramental or gnostic being will be the perfect consummation of the spiritual man.

In the Ignorance one is there primarily to grow, to know and to do, or, more exactly to grow into something, to arrive by knowledge at something, to get something done. Imperfect, we have no satisfaction of our being, we must perforce strive with labour and difficulty to grow into something we are not; ignorant and burdened with a consciousness of our ignorance, we have to arrive at something by which we can feel that we know; bounded with incapacity, we have to hunt after strength and power; afflicted with a consciousness of suffering, we have to try to get something done by which we catch at some pleasure or lay hold on some satisfying reality of life. To maintain existence is, indeed, our first occupation and necessity, but it is only a starting-point: for the mere maintenance of an imperfect existence chequered with suffering cannot be sufficient as an aim of our being; the instinctive will of existence, the pleasure of existence, which is all that the Ignorance can make out of the secret underlying Power and Ananda, has to be supplemented by the need to do and become. But what to do and what to become is not clearly known to us; we get what knowledge we can, what power, strength, purity, peace we can, what delight we can, become what we can. But our aims and our effort towards their achievement and the little we can hold as our gains turn into meshes by which we are bound; it is these things that become for us the object of life: to know our souls and to be our selves, which must be the foundation of our true way of being, is a secret that escapes us in our preoccupation with an external learning, an external construction of knowledge, the achievement of an external action, an external delight and pleasure. The spiritual man is one who has discovered his soul:

he has found his self and lives in that, is conscious of it, has the joy of it; he needs nothing external for his completeness of existence. The gnostic being starting from this new basis takes up our ignorant becoming and turns it into a luminous becoming of knowledge and a realised power of being. All therefore that is our attempt to be in the Ignorance, he will fulfil in the Knowledge. All knowledge he will turn into a manifestation of the self-knowledge of being, all power and action into a power and action of the self-force of being, all delight into a universal delight of self-existence. Attachment and bondage will fall away, because at each step and in each thing there will be the full satisfaction of self-existence, the light of the consciousness fulfilling itself, the ecstasy of delight of existence finding itself. Each stage of the evolution in the knowledge will be an unfolding of this power and will of being and this joy to be, a free becoming supported by the sense of the Infinite, the bliss of the Brahman,[22] the luminous sanction of the Transcendence.

The gnosis is the effective principle of the Spirit, a highest dynamis of the spiritual existence. The gnostic individual would be the consummation of the spiritual man; his whole way of being, thinking, living, acting would be governed by the power of a vast universal spirituality. All the trinities[23] of the Spirit would be real to his self-awareness and realised in his inner life. All his existence would be fused into oneness with the transcendent and universal Self and Spirit; all his action would originate from and obey the supreme Self and Spirit's divine governance of Nature. All life would have to him the sense of the Conscious Being, the Purusha[8] within, finding its self-expression in Nature; his life and all its thoughts, feelings, acts would be filled for him with that significance and built upon that foundation of its reality. He would feel the presence of the Divine in every centre of his consciousness, in every vibration of his life-force, in every cell of his body. In all the workings of his force of Nature he would be aware of the workings of the supreme World-Mother,[18] the Supernature; he would see his natural being as the becoming and manifestation of the power of the World-Mother. In this consciousness he would live and act in an entire transcendent freedom, a complete joy of the spirit, an entire identity with the cosmic Self and a spontaneous sympathy with all in the universe. All beings would be to him his own selves, all ways and powers of consciousness would be felt as the ways and powers of his own universality. But in that inclusive universality there would be no bondage to inferior forces, no deflection from his own highest truth: for this truth would envelop all truth of things and keep each in its own place, in a relation of diversified harmony, – it would not admit any confusion, clash, infringing of boundaries, any distortion of the different harmonies that constitute the total harmony. His own life and the world life would be to him like a perfect work of art; it would be as if the creation of a cosmic and spontaneous genius infallible in its working out of a multitudinous order. The gnostic individual would be in the world and of the world, but would also exceed it in his consciousness and live in his Self of transcendence above it; he would be universal but free in the universe, individual but not limited by a separative individuality. The True Person is not an isolated entity, his individuality is universal; for he individualises the universe: it is at the same time divinely emergent in a spiritual air of transcendental infinity, like a high cloud-surpassing summit; for he individual-ises the divine Transcendence. LD, 981-82, 971-73

The law of the Supermind is unity fulfilled in diversity; unity does not imply uniformity.

A supramental or gnostic race of beings would not be a race made according to a single type, moulded in a single fixed pattern; for the law of the Supermind is unity fulfilled in diversity, and therefore there would be an infinite diversity in the manifestation of the gnostic consciousness although that consciousness would still be one in its basis, in its constitution, in its all-revealing and all-uniting order.... In the supramental race itself, in the variation of its degrees, the individuals would not be cast according to a single type of individuality; each would be different from the other, a unique formation of the Being, although one with all the rest in foundation of self and sense of oneness and in the principle of his being.

In the lower grades of gnostic being, there would be a limitation of self-expression according to the variety of the nature, a limited perfection in order to formulate some side, element or combined harmony of elements of some Divine Totality, a restricted selection of powers from the cosmic figure of the infinitely manifold One. But in the supramental being this need of limitation for perfection would disappear; the diversity would not be secured by limitation but by a diversity in the power and hue of the Supernature: the same whole of being and the same whole of nature would express themselves in an infinitely diverse fashion; for each being would be a new totality, harmony, self-equation of the One Being. What would be expressed in front or held behind at any moment would depend not on capacity or incapacity, but on the dynamic self-choice of the Spirit, its delight of self-expression, on the truth of the Divine's will and joy of itself in the individual and, subordinately, on the truth of the thing that had to be done through the individual in the harmony of the totality. For the complete individual is the cosmic individual, since only when we have taken the universe into ourselves – and transcended it, – can our individuality be complete.   LD, 971, 973-74

The supramental being will realise the harmony of his individual self with the cosmic Self, of his individual will and action with the cosmic Will and Action.

The supramental being in his cosmic consciousness seeing and feeling all as himself would act in that sense; he would act in a universal awareness and a harmony of his individual self with the total self, of his individual will with the total will, of his individual action with the total action. For what we most suffer from in our outer life and its reactions upon our inner life is the imperfection of our relations with the world, our ignorance of others, our disharmony with the whole of things, our inability to equate our demand on the world with the world's demand on us. There is a conflict, – a conflict from which there seems to be no ultimate issue except an escape from both world and self, – between our self-affirmation and a world on which we have to impose that affirmation, a world which seems to be too large for us and to pass indifferently over our soul, mind, life, body in the sweep of its course to its goal. The relation of our course and goal to the world's is unapparent to us, and to harmonise ourselves with it we have either to enforce ourselves upon it and make it subservient to us or suppress ourselves and become subservient to it or else to compass a difficult balance between these two necessities of the relation between the individual personal destiny and the cosmic whole and its hidden purpose. But for the supramental being living in a cosmic consciousness the difficulty would not exist, since he has no ego; his cosmic individuality would know the cosmic forces and their movement and their significance as part of himself, and the truth-consciousness in him would see the right relation at each step and find the dynamic right expression of that relation.

For in fact both individual and universe are simultaneous and interrelated expressions of the same transcendent Being....

One in self with all, the supramental being will seek the delight of self-manifestation of the Spirit in himself but equally the delight of the Divine in all: he will have the cosmic joy and will be a power for bringing the bliss of the Spirit, the joy of being to others; for their joy will be part of his own joy of existence. To be occupied with the good of all beings, to make the joy and grief of others one's own has been described as a sign of the liberated and fulfilled spiritual man. The supramental being will have no need for that, of an altruistic self-effacement, since this occupation will be intimate to his self-fulfilment, the fulfilment of the One in all, and there will be no contradiction or strife between his own good and the good of others: nor will he have any need to acquire a universal sympathy by subjecting himself to the joys and griefs of creatures in the Ignorance; his cosmic sympathy will be part of his inborn truth of being and not dependent on a personal participation in the lesser joy and suffering; it will transcend what it embraces and in that transcendence will be its power. His feeling of universality, his action of universality will be always a spontaneous state and natural movement, an automatic expression of the Truth, an act of the joy of the Spirit's self-existence. There could be in it no place for limited self or desire or for the satisfaction or frustration of the limited self or the satisfaction or frustration of desire, no place for the relative and dependent happiness and grief that visit and afflict our limited nature; for these are things that belong to the ego and the Ignorance, not to the freedom and truth of the Spirit.... The gnostic existence and delight of existence is a universal and total being and delight, and there will be the presence of that totality and universality in each separate movement: in each there will be, not a partial experience of self or fractional bit of its joy, but the sense of the whole movement of an integral being and the presence of its entire and integral bliss of being, Ananda.[2]   LD, 974, 975-77

The transcendence aspect of the spiritual life is indispensable for the freedom of the Spirit; but it will harmonise with the manifested existence and give it an unshakable foundation. For the gnostic being, to act in the world does not signify a lapse from unity.

The gnostic life will be an inner life in which the antinomy of the inner and the outer, the self and the world will have been cured and exceeded. The gnostic being will have indeed an inmost existence in which he is alone with God, one with the Eternal, self-plunged into the depths of the Infinite, in communion with its heights and its luminous abysses of secrecy; nothing will be able to disturb or to invade these depths or bring him down from the summits, neither the world's contents nor his action nor all that is around him. This is the transcendence-aspect of the spiritual life and it is necessary for the freedom of the Spirit; for otherwise the identity in Nature with the world would be a binding limitation and not a free identity. But at the same time God-love and the delight of God will be the heart's expression of that inner communion and oneness, and that delight and love will expand itself to embrace all existence. The peace of God within will be extended in the gnostic experience of the universe into a universal calm of equality not merely passive but dynamic, a calm of freedom in oneness dominating all that meets it, tranquillising all that enters into it, imposing its law of peace on the supramental being's relations with the world in which he is living. Into all his acts the inner oneness, the inner communion will attend him and enter into his relations with others, who will not be to him others but selves of himself in the one existence, his own universal existence. It is this poise and freedom in the Spirit that will enable him to take all life into himself while still remaining the spiritual self and to embrace even the world of the Ignorance without himself entering into the Ignorance.

The gnostic being has the will of action but also the knowledge of what is to be willed and the power to effectuate its knowledge; it will not be led from ignorance to do what is not to be done. Moreover, its action is not the seeking for a fruit or result; its joy is in being and doing, in pure state of Spirit, in pure act of Spirit, in the pure bliss of the Spirit.... The gnostic being's knowledge self-realised in action will be, not an ideative knowledge, but the Real-Idea[24] of the Supermind, the instrumentation of an essential light of Consciousness; it will be the self-light of all the reality of being and becoming pouring itself out continually and filling every particular act and activity with the pure and whole delight of its self-existence. For an infinite consciousness with its knowledge by identity there is in each differentiation the joy and experience of the Identical, in each finite is felt the Infinite.   LD, 978-79, 976-77

The gnostic consciousness will proceed towards an integral knowledge. And that will not be a revelation or a delivery of light out of darkness, but of light out of light.

Mind seeks for light, for knowledge, – for knowledge of the one truth basing all, an essential truth of self and things, but also of all truth of diversity of that oneness, all its detail, circumstance, manifold way of action, form, law of movement and happening, various manifestation and creation; for thinking mind the joy of existence is discovery and the penetration of the mystery of creation that comes with knowledge. This the gnostic change will fulfil in an ample measure; but it will give it a new character. It will act not by the discovery of the unknown, but by the bringing out of the known; all will be the finding "of the self by the self in the self "

A replacement of intellectual seeking by supramental identity and gnostic intuition of the contents of the identity, an omnipresence of Spirit with its light penetrating the whole process of knowledge and all its use, – so that there is an integration between the knower, knowledge and the thing known, between the operating consciousness, the instrumentation and the thing done, while the single self watches over the whole integrated movement and fulfils itself intimately in it, making it a flawless unit of self-effectuation, – will be the character of each gnostic movement of knowledge and action of knowledge. Mind, observing and reasoning, labours to detach itself and see objectively and truly what it has to know; it tries to know it as not-self, independent other-reality not affected by process of personal thinking or by any presence of self: the gnostic consciousness will at once intimately and exactly know its object by a comprehending and penetrating identification with it. It will overpass what it has to know, but it will include it in itself; it will know the object as part of itself as it might know any part or movement of its own being, without any narrowing of itself by the identification or snaring of its thought in it so as to be bound or limited in knowledge. There will be the intimacy, accuracy, fullness of a direct internal knowledge, but not that misleading by personal mind by which we constantly err, because the consciousness will be that of a universal and not a restricted and ego-bound person. It will proceed towards all knowledge, not setting truth against truth to see which will stand and survive, but completing truth by truth in the light of the one Truth of which all are the aspects.... There will be an unfolding, not as a delivery of light out of darkness, but as a delivery of light out of itself; for if an evolving supramental Consciousness holds back part of its contents of self-awareness behind in itself, it does this not as a step or by an act of Ignorance, but as the movement of a deliberate bringing out of its timeless knowledge into a process of Time-manifestation.

LD, 982, 983-84

The joy of an intimate self-revealing diversity of the One, the multitudinous union and happy interaction within the One, will give a fully perfected sense to the gnostic life.

As mind seeks for light, for the discovery of knowledge and for mastery by knowledge, so life seeks for the development of its own force and for mastery by force: its quest is for growth, power, conquest, possession, satisfaction, creation, joy, love, beauty; its joy of existence is in a constant self-expression, development, diverse manifoldness of action, creation, enjoyment, an abundant and strong intensity of itself and its power. The gnostic evolution will lift that to its highest and fullest expression, but it will not act for the power, satisfaction, enjoyment of the mental or vital ego, for its narrow possession of itself and its eager ambitious grasp on others and on things or for its greater self-affirmation and magnified embodiment; for in that way no spiritual fullness and perfection can come. The gnostic life will exist and act for the Divine in itself and in the world, for the Divine in all; the increasing possession of the individual being and the world by the Divine Presence, Light, Power, Love, Delight, Beauty will be the sense of life to the gnostic being. In the more and more perfect satisfaction of that growing manifestation will be the individual's satisfaction: his power will be the instrumentation of the power of Supernature for bringing in and extending that greater life and nature; whatever conquest and adventure will be there, will be for that only and not for the reign of any individual or collective ego. Love will be for him the contact, meeting, union of self with self, of spirit with spirit, a unification of being, a power and joy and intimacy and closeness of soul to soul, of the One to the One, a joy of identity and the consequences of a diverse identity. It is this joy of an intimate self-revealing diversity of the One, the multitudinous union of the One and a happy interaction in the identity, that will be for him the full revealed sense of life. Creation aesthetic or dynamic, mental creation, life creation, material creation will have for him the same sense. It will be the creation of significant forms of the Eternal Force, Light, Beauty, Reality, – the beauty and truth of its forms and bodies, the beauty and truth of its powers and qualities, the beauty and truth of its spirit, its formless beauty of self and essence.

As a consequence of the total change and reversal of consciousness establishing a new relation of Spirit with Mind and Life and Matter, and a new significance and perfection in the relation, there will be a reversal, a perfecting new significance also of the relations between the spirit and the body it inhabits.   LD, 984-85

> *Matter will reveal itself as an instrument of the manifestation of Spirit; a new liberated and sovereign acceptance of material Nature will then be possible.*

This new relation of the Spirit and the body assumes, – and makes possible, – a free acceptance of the whole of material Nature in place of a rejection; the drawing back from her, the refusal of all identification or acceptance, which is the first normal necessity of the spiritual consciousness for its liberation, is no longer imperative. To cease to be identified with the body, to separate oneself from the body-consciousness, is a recognised and necessary step whether towards spiritual liberation or towards spiritual perfection and mastery over Nature. But, this redemption once effected, the descent of the spiritual light and force can invade and take up the body also and there can be a new liberated and sovereign acceptance of material Nature. That is possible, indeed, only if there is a changed communion of the Spirit with Matter, a control, a reversal of the present balance of interaction which allows physical Nature to veil the Spirit and affirm her own dominance. In the light of a larger knowledge Matter also can be seen to be the Brahman,[22] a self-energy put forth by the Brahman, a form and substance of Brahman; aware of the secret consciousness within material substance, secure in this larger knowledge, the gnostic light and power can unite itself with Matter, so seen, and accept it as an instrument of a spiritual manifestation. A certain reverence, even, for Matter and a sacramental attitude in all dealings with it is possible.... The gnostic being, using Matter but using it without material or vital attachment or desire, will feel that he is using the Spirit in this form of itself with its consent and sanction for its own purpose. There will be in him a certain respect for physical things, an awareness of the occult consciousness in them, of its dumb will of utility and service, a worship of the Divine, the Brahman in what he uses, a care for a perfect and faultless use of his divine material, for a true rhythm, ordered harmony, beauty in the life of Matter, in the utilisation of Matter.   LD, 986-87

*The body will become a faithful and capable instrument,
perfectly responsive to the Spirit.*

For the law of the body arises from the subconscient or inconscient: but in the gnostic being the subconscient will have become conscious and subject to the supramental control, penetrated with its light and action; the basis of inconscience with its obscurity and ambiguity, its obstruction or tardy responses will have been transformed into a lower or supporting superconscience by the supramental emergence. Already even in the realised higher-mind being and in the intuitive and overmind being the body will have become sufficiently conscious to respond to the influence of the Idea[24] and the Will-Force so that the action of mind on the physical parts, which is rudimentary, chaotic and mostly involuntary in us, will have developed a considerable potency: but in the supramental being it is the consciousness with the Real-Idea[24] in it which will govern everything. This Real-Idea is a truth-perception which is self-effective; for it is the idea and will of the Spirit in direct action and originates a movement of the substance of being which must inevitably effectuate itself in state and act of being. It is this dynamic irresistible spiritual realism of the Truth-Consciousness in the highest degree of itself that will have here grown conscient and consciously competent in the evolved gnostic being: it will not act as now, veiled in an apparent inconscience and self-limited by law of mechanism, but as the sovereign Reality in self-effectuating action. It is this that will rule the existence with an entire knowledge and power and include in its rule the functioning and action of the body. The body will be turned by the power of the spiritual consciousness into a true and fit and perfectly responsive instrument of the Spirit.   LD, 985-86

> *Health, strength, duration, bodily happiness and ease,*
> *liberation from suffering, are a part of the physical perfection*
> *which the gnostic evolution is called upon to realise.*

As a result of this new relation between the Spirit and the body, the gnostic evolution will effectuate the spiritualisation, perfection and fulfilment of the physical being; it will do for the body as for the mind and life. Apart from the obscurity, frailties and limitations, which this change will overcome, the body-consciousness is a patient servant and can be in its large reserve of possibilities a potent instrument of the individual life, and it asks for little on its own account: what it craves for is duration, health, strength, physical perfection, bodily happiness, liberation from suffering, ease. These demands are not in themselves unacceptable, mean or illegitimate, for they render into the terms of Matter the perfection of form and substance, the power and delight which should be the natural outflowing, the expressive manifestation of the Spirit. When the gnostic Force can act in the body, these things can be established; for their opposites come from a pressure of external forces on the physical mind, on the nervous and material life, on the body-organism, from an ignorance that does not know how to meet these forces or is not able to meet them rightly or with power, and from some obscurity, pervading the stuff of the physical consciousness and distorting its responses, that reacts to them in a wrong way.

It is the incompleteness and weakness of the Consciousness-Force manifested in the mental, vital and physical being, its inability to receive or refuse at will, or, receiving, to assimilate or harmonise the contacts of the universal Energy cast upon it, that is the cause of pain and suffering. In the material realm Nature starts with an entire insensibility, and it is a notable fact that either a comparative insensibility or a deficient sensibility or more often, a greater endurance and hardness to suffering is found in the beginnings of life, in the animal, in primitive or less developed man; as the human being grows in evolution, he grows in sensibility and suffers more keenly in mind and life and body. For the growth in consciousness is not sufficiently supported by a growth in force; the body becomes more subtle, more finely capable, but less solidly efficient in its external energy: man has to call in his will, his mental power to dynamise, correct and control his nervous being, force it to the strenuous tasks he demands from his instruments, steel it against suffering and disaster. In the spiritual ascent this power of the consciousness and its will over the instruments, the control of spirit and inner mind over the outer mentality and the nervous being and the body, increases immensely; a tranquil and wide equality of the spirit to all shocks and contacts comes in and becomes the habitual poise, and this can pass from the mind to the vital parts and establish there too an immense and enduring largeness of strength and peace; even in the body this state may form itself and meet inwardly the shocks of grief and pain and all kinds of suffering. Even, a power of willed physical insensibility can intervene or a power of mental separation from all shock and injury can be acquired which shows that the ordinary reactions and the debile submission of the bodily self to the normal habits of response of material Nature are not obligatory or unalterable. Still more significant is the power that comes on the level of spiritual mind or Overmind to change the vibrations of pain into vibrations of Ananda[2]: even if this were to go only up to a certain point, it indicates the possibility of an entire reversal of the ordinary rule of the reacting consciousness; it can be associated too with a power of self-protection that turns away the shocks that are more difficult to transmute or to endure. The gnostic evolution at a certain stage must bring about a completeness of this reversal and of this power of self-protection which will fulfil the claim of the body for immunity and serenity of its being and for deliverance from suffering and build in it a power for the total delight of existence. A spiritual Ananda can flow into the body and inundate cell and tissue; a luminous materialisation of this higher Ananda could of itself bring about a total transformation of the deficient or adverse sensibilities of physical Nature.   LD, 987-89

> *A vast calm and a deep delight of the gnostic existence rise together in a growing intensity and culminate in an eternal ecstasy. In the universal phenomenon is revealed the eternal Bliss, Ananda.*

An aspiration, a demand for the supreme and total delight of existence is there secretly in the whole make of our being, but it is disguised by the separation of our parts of nature and their differing urge and obscured by their inability to conceive or seize anything more than a superficial pleasure. In the body-consciousness this demand takes shape as a need of bodily happiness, in our life parts as a yearning for life happiness, a keen vibrant response to joy and rapture of many kinds and to all surprise of satisfaction; in the mind it shapes into a ready reception of all forms of mental delight; on a higher level it becomes apparent in the spiritual mind's call for peace and divine ecstasy. This trend is founded in the truth of the being; for Ananda[2] is the very essence of the Brahman, it is the supreme nature of the omnipresent Reality. The supermind itself in the descending degrees of the manifestation emerges from the Ananda and in the evolutionary ascent merges into the Ananda. It is not, indeed, merged in the sense of being extinguished or abolished but is there inherent in it, indistinguishable from the self of awareness and the self-effectuating force of the Bliss of Being. In the involutionary descent as in the evolutionary return supermind is supported by the original Delight of Existence and carries that in it in all its activities as their sustaining essence; for Consciousness, we may say, is its parent power in the Spirit, but Ananda is the spiritual matrix from which it manifests and the maintaining source into which it carries back the soul in its return to the status of the Spirit. A supramental manifestation in its ascent would have as a next sequence and culmination of self-result a manifestation of the Bliss of the Brahman: the evolution of the being of gnosis would be followed by an evolution of the being of bliss; an embodiment of gnostic existence would have as its consequence an embodiment of the beatific existence.... In the liberation of the soul from the Ignorance the first foundation is peace, calm, the silence and quietude of the Eternal and Infinite; but a consummate power and greater formation of the spiritual ascension takes up this peace of liberation into the bliss of a perfect experience and realisation of the eternal beatitude, the bliss of the Eternal and Infinite.

Peace and ecstasy cease to be different and become one. The supermind, reconciling and fusing all differences as well as all contradictions, brings out this unity; a wide calm and a deep delight of all-existence are among its first steps of self-realisation, but this calm and this delight rise together, as one state, into an increasing intensity and culminate in the eternal ecstasy, the bliss that is the Infinite. In the gnostic consciousness at any stage there would be always in some degree this fundamental and spiritual conscious delight of existence in the whole depth of the being; but also all the movements of Nature would be pervaded by it, and all the actions and reactions of the life and the body: none could escape the law of the Ananda. Even before the gnostic change there can be a beginning of this fundamental ecstasy of being translated into a manifold beauty and delight. In the mind, it translates into a calm of intense delight of spiritual perception and vision and knowledge, in the heart into a wide or deep or passionate delight of universal union and love and sympathy and the joy of beings and the joy of things. In the will and vital parts it is felt as the energy of delight of a divine life-power in action or a beatitude of the senses perceiving and meeting the One everywhere, perceiving as their normal aesthesis of things a universal beauty and a secret harmony of creation of which our mind can catch only imperfect glimpses or a rare supernormal sense. In the body it reveals itself as ecstasy pouring into it from the heights of the spirit and the peace and bliss of a pure and spiritualised physical existence. A universal beauty and glory of being begins to manifest; all objects reveal hidden lines, vibrations, powers, harmonic significances concealed from the normal mind and the physical sense. In the universal phenomenon is revealed the eternal Ananda.   LD, 989-90, 991

Two questions remain to be examined, which are important for the human conception of life.

1. What is the place of personality in the gnostic being?

Ordinarily, in the common notion, the separative ego is our self and, if ego has to disappear in a transcendental or universal Consciousness, personal life and action must cease; for, the individual disappearing, there can only be an impersonal consciousness, a cosmic self: but if the individual is altogether extinguished, no further question of personality or responsibility or ethical perfection can arise. According to another line of ideas the spiritual person remains, but liberated, purified, perfected in nature in a celestial existence. But here we are still on earth, and yet it is supposed that the ego personality is extinguished and replaced by a universalised spiritual individual who is a centre and power of the transcendent Being. It might be deduced that this gnostic or supramental individual is a self without personality, an impersonal Purusha. There could be many gnostic individuals but there would be no personality, all would be the same in being and nature.   LD, 992

In the gnostic consciousness personality and impersonality are not opposing principles; they are inseparable aspects of one and the same reality.

This reality is not the ego but the being, who is impersonal and universal in his stuff of nature, but forms out of it an expressive personality which is his form of self in the changes of Nature.

The Divine, the Eternal, expresses himself as existence, consciousness, bliss, wisdom, knowledge, love, beauty, and we can think of him as these impersonal and universal powers of himself, regard them as the nature of the Divine and Eternal; we can say that God is Love, God is Wisdom, God is Truth or Righteousness: but he is not himself an impersonal state or abstract of states or qualities; he is the Being, at once absolute, universal and individual. If we look at it from this basis, there is, very clearly, no opposition, no incompatibility, no impossibility of a co-existence or one-existence of the Impersonal and the Person; they are each other, live in one another, melt into each other, and yet in a way can appear as if different ends, sides, obverse and reverse of the same Reality. The gnostic being is of the nature of the Divine and therefore repeats in himself this natural mystery of existence.

LD, 992-93, 993-94

What will be the nature of the gnostic person?

The ordinary restricted personality can be grasped by a description of the characters stamped on its life and thought and action, its very definite surface building and expression of self.... But such a description would be pitifully inadequate to express the Person when its Power of Self within manifests more amply and puts forward its hidden daemonic force in the surface composition and the life. We feel ourselves in presence of a light of consciousness, a potency, a sea of energy, can distinguish and describe its free waves of action and quality, but not fix itself; and yet there is an impression of personality, the presence of a powerful being, a strong, high or beautiful recognisable Someone, a Person, not a limited creature of Nature but a Self or Soul, a Purusha.[8] The gnostic Individual would be such an inner Person unveiled, occupying both the depths, – no longer self-hidden, – and the surface in a unified self-awareness; he would not be a surface personality partly expressive of a larger secret being, he would be not the wave but the ocean: he would be the Purusha, the inner conscious Existence self-revealed, and would have no need of a carved expressive mask or *persona*.

This, then, would be the nature of the gnostic Person, an infinite and universal being revealing, – or, to our mental ignorance, suggesting, – its eternal self through the significant form and expressive power of an individual and temporal self-manifestation. But the individual nature-manifestation, whether strong and distinct in outline or multitudinous and protean but still harmonic, would be there as an index of the being, not as the whole being: that would be felt behind, recognisable but indefinable, infinite. The consciousness also of the gnostic Person would be an infinite consciousness throwing up forms of self-expression, but aware always of its unbound infinity and universality and conveying the power and sense of its infinity and universality even in the finiteness of the expression, – by which, moreover, it would not be bound in the next movement of farther self-revelation. But this would still not be an unregulated un-recognisable flux but a process of self-revelation making visible the inherent truth of its powers of existence according to the harmonic law natural to all manifestation of the Infinite.   LD, 995-96

> 2. *If there is a gnostic personality and if it is in some way responsible for its acts, what is the place of the ethical element in the gnostic nature, what is its perfection and its fulfilment?*

... the law, the standard has to be imposed on us now because there is in our natural being an opposite force of separateness, a possibility of antagonism, a force of discord, ill-will, strife. All ethics is a construction of good in a Nature which has been smitten with evil by the powers of darkness born of the Ignorance, even as it is expressed in the ancient legend of the Vedanta.[25] But where all is self-determined by truth of consciousness and truth of being, there can be no standard, no struggle to observe it, no virtue or merit, no sin or demerit of the nature. The power of love, of truth, of right will be there, not as a law mentally constructed but as the very substance and constitution of the nature and, by the integration of the being, necessarily also the very stuff and constituting nature of the action. To grow into this nature of our being, a nature of spiritual truth and oneness, is the liberation attained by an evolution of the spiritual being: the gnostic evolution gives us the complete dynamism of that return to ourselves. Once that is done, the need of standards of virtue, *dharmas*,[10] disappears;

there is the law and self-order of the liberty of the spirit, there can be no imposed or constructed law of conduct, dharma. All becomes a self-flow of spiritual self-nature, Swadharma of Swabhava.[26]   LD, 997-98

> *The gnostic life will reconcile freedom and order. There will be an entire accord between the free expression of the individual and his obedience to the inherent law of the supreme and universal Truth of things.*

A separate self-existent being could be at odds with other separate beings, at variance with the universal All in which they co-exist, in a state of contradiction with any supreme Truth that was willing its self-expression in the universe; this is what happens to the individual in the Ignorance, because he takes his stand on the consciousness of a separate individuality. There can be a similar conflict, discord, disparity between the truths, the energies, qualities, powers, modes of being that act as separate forces in the individual and in the universe. A world full of conflict, a conflict in ourselves, a conflict of the individual with the world around him are normal and inevitable features of the separative consciousness of the Ignorance and our ill-harmonised existence. But this cannot happen in the gnostic consciousness because there each finds his complete self and all find their own truth and the harmony of their different motions in that which exceeds them and of which they are the expression. In the gnostic life, therefore, there is an entire accord between the free self-expression of the being and his automatic obedience to the inherent law of the supreme and universal Truth of things. These are to him interconnected sides of the one Truth; it is his own supreme truth of being which works itself out in the whole united truth of himself and things in one Supernature.

The two principles of freedom and order, which in mind and life are constantly representing themselves as contraries or incompatibles, though they have no need to be that if freedom is guarded by knowledge and order based upon truth of being, are in the supermind consciousness native to each other and even fundamentally one. This is so because both are inseparable aspects of the inner spiritual truth and therefore their determinations are one; they are inherent in each other, for they arise from an identity and therefore in action coincide in a natural identity. The gnostic being does not in any way or degree feel his liberty infringed by the imperative order of his thought or actions, because that order is intrinsic and spontaneous; he feels both his liberty and the order of his liberty to be one truth of his being. His liberty of knowledge is not a freedom to follow falsehood or error, for he does not need like the mind to pass through the possibility of error in order to know, – on the contrary, any such deviation would be a departure from his plenitude of the gnostic self, it would be a diminution of his self-truth and alien and injurious to his being; for his freedom is a freedom of light, not of darkness. His liberty of action is not a licence to act upon wrong will or the impulsions of the Ignorance, for that too would be alien to his being, a restriction and diminution of it, not a liberation. A drive for fulfilment of falsehood or wrong will would be felt by him, not as a movement towards freedom, but as a violence done to the liberty of the Spirit, an invasion and imposition, an inroad upon his Supernature, a tyranny of some alien Nature.

A similar inevitability of the union of freedom and order would be the law of the collective life; it would be a freedom of the diverse play of the Infinite in divine souls, an order of the conscious unity of souls which is the law of the supramental Infinite. Our mental rendering of oneness brings into it the rule of sameness; a complete oneness brought about by the mental reason drives towards a thoroughgoing standardisation as its one effective means, – only minor shades of differentiation would be allowed to operate: but the greatest richness of diversity in the self-expression of oneness would be the law of the gnostic life. In the gnostic consciousness difference would not lead to discord but to a spontaneous natural adaptation, a sense of complementary plenitude, a rich many-sided execution of the thing to be collectively known, done, worked out in life.

LD, 999-1000, 1003-04, 1010

*All mental standards would disappear because their neces-
sity would cease; the authentic law of identity with the
Divine Self would have replaced them.*

On this fact that the Divine Knowledge and Force, the supreme Supernature, would act through the gnostic being with his full participation, is founded the freedom of the gnostic being; it is this unity that gives him his liberty. The freedom from law, including the moral law, so frequently affirmed of the spiritual being, is founded on this unity of its will with the will of the Eternal. All the mental standards would disappear because all necessity for them would cease; the higher authentic law of identity with the Divine Self and identity with all beings would have replaced them. There would be no question of selfishness or altruism, of oneself and others, since all are seen and felt as the one self and only what the supreme Truth and Good decided would be done. There would be in the action a pervasive feeling of a self-existent universal love, sympathy, oneness, but the feeling would penetrate, colour and move in the act, not solely dominate or determine it: it would not stand for itself in opposition to the larger truth of things or dictate a personally impelled departure from the divinely willed true movement. This opposition and departure can happen in the Ignorance where love or any other strong principle of the nature can be divorced from wisdom even as it can be divorced from power; but in the supermind gnosis all powers are intimate to each other and act as one. In the gnostic person the Truth-Knowledge would lead and determine and all the other forces of the being concur in the action: there would be no place for disharmony or conflict between the powers of the nature.

LD, 1006

CHAPTER IX

The Divine Life upon Earth

> *To be wholly and integrally conscious of oneself and of all the truth of one's being is what is implied by the perfect emergence of the individual consciousness, and it is that towards which evolution tends. All being is one, and to be fully conscious means to be integrated with the consciousness of all, with the universal self and force and action.*

For the essence of consciousness is the power to be aware of itself and its objects, and in its true nature this power must be direct, self-fulfilled and complete: if it is in us indirect, incomplete, unfulfilled in its workings, dependent on constructed instruments, it is because consciousness here is emerging from an original veiling Inconscience and is yet burdened and enveloped with the first Nescience proper to the Inconscient; but it must have the power to emerge completely, its destiny must be to evolve into its own perfection which is its true nature. Its true nature is to be wholly aware of its objects, and of these objects the first is self, the being which is evolving its consciousness here, and the rest is what we see as not-self, – but if existence is indivisible, that too must in reality be self: the destiny of evolving consciousness must be, then, to become perfect in its awareness, entirely aware of self and all-aware. This perfect and natural condition of consciousness is to us a superconscience, a state which is beyond us and in which our mind, if suddenly transferred to it, could not at first function; but it is towards that superconscience that our conscious being must be evolving. But this evolution of our consciousness to a superconscience or supreme of itself is possible only if the Inconscience which is our basis here is really itself an involved Superconscience; for what is to be in the becoming of the Reality in us must be already there involved or secret in its beginning. Such an involved Being or Power we can well conceive the Inconscient to be when we closely regard this material creation of an unconscious Energy and see it labouring out with curious construction and infinite device the work of a vast involved Intelligence and see, too, that we ourselves are something of that Intelligence evolving out of its involution, an emerging consciousness whose emergence cannot stop short on the way until the Involved has evolved and revealed itself as a supreme totally self-aware and all-aware Intelligence. It is this to which we have given the name of Supermind[9] or Gnosis. For that evidently must be the consciousness of the Reality, the Being, the Spirit that is secret in us and slowly manifesting here; of that Being we are the becomings and must grow into its nature.

To be and to be fully is Nature's aim in us; but to be fully is to be wholly conscious of one's being: unconsciousness, half consciousness or deficient consciousness is a state of being not in possession of itself; it is existence, but not fullness of being. To be aware wholly and integrally of oneself and of all the truth of one's being is the necessary condition of true possession of existence. This self-awareness is what is meant by spiritual knowledge: the essence of spiritual knowledge is an intrinsic self-existent consciousness; all its action of knowledge, indeed all its action of any kind, must be that consciousness formulating itself. All other knowledge is consciousness oblivious of itself and striving to return to its own awareness of itself and its contents; it is self-ignorance labouring to transform itself back into self-knowledge.

To become complete in being, in consciousness of being, in force of being, in delight of being and to live in this integrated completeness is the divine living.

All being is one and to be fully is to be all that is. To be in the being of all and to include all in one's being, to be conscious of the consciousness of all, to be integrated in force with the universal force, to carry all action and experience in oneself and feel it as one's own action and experience, to feel all selves as one's self, to feel all delight of being as one's own delight of being is a necessary condition of the integral divine living.

LD, 1017, 1023-24, 1025

The plenitude of this consciousness can only be attained by realising the identity of the individual self with the transcendent Self, the supreme Reality.

But thus to be universally in the fullness and freedom of one's universality, one must be also transcendentally. The spiritual fullness of the being is eternity; if one has not the consciousness of timeless eternal being, if one is dependent on body or embodied mind or embodied life, or dependent on this world or that world or on this condition of being or that condition of being, that is not the reality of self, not the fullness of our spiritual existence. To live only as a self of body or be only by the body is to be an ephemeral creature, subject to death and desire and pain and suffering and decay and decadence. To transcend, to exceed consciousness of body, not to be held in the body or by the body, to hold the body only as an instrument, a minor outward formation of self, is a first condition of divine living. Not to be a mind subject to ignorance and restriction of consciousness, to transcend mind and handle it as an instrument, to control it as a surface formation of self, is a second condition. To be by the self and Spirit, not to depend upon life, not to be identified with it, to transcend it and control and use it as an expression and instrumentation of the self, is a third condition.

[The individual] must enter into the supreme divine Reality, feel his oneness with it, live in it, be its self-creation: all his mind, life, physicality must be converted into terms of its Supernature; all his thoughts, feelings, actions must be determined by it and be it, its self-formation. All this can become complete in him only when he has evolved out of the Ignorance into the

Knowledge and through the Knowledge into the supreme Consciousness and its dynamis and supreme delight of existence; but some essentiality of these things and their sufficient instrumentation can come with the first spiritual change and culminate in the life of the gnostic supernature.[8]   LD, 1025-26

This realisation demands a turning of the consciousness inward. The ordinary human consciousness is turned outward and sees the surface of things only. It recoils from entering the inner depths which appear dark and where it is afraid of losing itself. Yet the entry into this obscurity, this void, this silence is only the passage to a greater existence.

These things are impossible without an inward living; they cannot be reached by remaining in an external consciousness turned always outwards, active only or mainly on and from the surface. The individual being has to find himself, his true existence; he can only do this by going inward, by living within and from within....

This movement of going inward and living inward is a difficult task to lay upon the normal consciousness of the human being; yet there is no other way of self-finding. The materialistic thinker, erecting an opposition between the extrovert and the introvert, holds up the extrovert attitude for acceptance as the only safety: to go inward is to enter into darkness or emptiness or to lose the balance of the consciousness and become morbid; it is from outside that such inner life as one can construct is created, and its health is assured only by a strict reliance on its wholesome and nourishing outer sources, – the balance of the personal mind and life can only be secured by a firm support on external reality, for the material world is the sole fundamental reality. This may be true for the physical man, the born extrovert, who feels himself to be a creature of outward Nature; made by her and dependent on her, he would lose himself if he went inward: for him there is no inner being, no inner living.

But the introvert of this distinction also has not the inner life; he is not a seer of the true inner self and of inner things, but the small mental man who looks superficially inside himself and sees there not his spiritual self but his life-ego, his mind-ego and becomes unhealthily preoccupied with the movements of this little pitiful dwarf creature. The idea or experience of an inner darkness when looking inwards is the first reaction of a mentality which has lived always on the surface and has no realised inner existence; it has only a constructed internal experience which depends on the outside world for the materials of its being. But to those into whose composition there has entered the power of a more inner living, the movement of going within and living within brings not a darkness or dull emptiness but an enlargement, a rush of new experience, a greater vision, a larger capacity, an extended life infinitely more real and various than the first pettiness of the life constructed for itself by our normal physical humanity, a joy of being which is larger and richer than any delight in existence than the outer vital man or the surface mental man can gain by their dynamic vital force and activity or subtlety and expansion of the mental existence. A silence, an entry into a wide or even immense or infinite emptiness is part of the inner spiritual experience; of this silence and void the physical mind has a certain fear, the small superficially active thinking or vital mind a shrinking from it or dislike, – for it confuses the silence with mental and vital incapacity and the void with cessation or non-existence: but this silence is the silence of the spirit which is the condition of a greater knowledge, power and bliss, and this emptiness is the emptying of the cup of our natural being, a liberation of it from its turbid contents so that it may be filled with the wine of God; it is the passage not into non-existence but to a greater existence. Even when the being turns towards cessation, it is a cessation not in non-existence but into some vast ineffable of spiritual being or the plunge into the incommunicable super-conscience of the Absolute.   LD, 1027-29

Indeed, this inward-turning movement is not an imprison-
ment in the personal self; it is the first step towards a true
universality.

In fact, this inward turning and movement is not an imprisonment in personal self, it is the first step towards a true
universality; it brings to us the truth of our external as well as
the truth of our internal existence. For this inner living can
extend itself and embrace the universal life, it can contact,
penetrate, englobe the life of all with a much greater reality and
dynamic force than is in our surface consciousness at all
possible. Our outmost universalisation on the surface is a poor
and limping endeavour, – it is a construction, a make-believe
and not the real thing: for in our surface consciousness we are
bound to separation of consciousness from others and wear the
fetters of the ego. There our very selflessness becomes more
often than not a subtle form of selfishness or turns into a larger
affirmation of our ego; content with our pose of altruism, we do
not see that it is a veil for the imposition of our individual self,
our ideas, our mental and vital personality, our need of ego-
enlargement upon the others whom we take up into our
expanded orbit. So far as we really succeed in living for others,
it is done by an inner spiritual force of love and sympathy; but
the power and field of effectuality of this force in us are small,
the psychic movement that prompts it is incomplete, its action
often ignorant because there is contact of mind and heart but
our being does not embrace the being of others as ourselves. An
external unity with others must always be an outward joining
and association of external lives with a minor inner result; the
mind and heart attach their movements to this common life and
the beings whom we meet there; but the common external life
remains the foundation, – the inward constructed unity, or so
much of it as can persist in spite of mutual ignorance and
discordant egoisms, conflict of minds, conflict of hearts, conflict
of vital temperaments, conflict of interests, is a partial and
insecure superstructure. The spiritual consciousness, the spiritual life reverses this principle of building; it bases its action in

the collective life upon an inner experience and inclusion of others in our own being, an inner sense and reality of oneness. The spiritual individual acts out of that sense of oneness which gives him immediate and direct perception of the demand of self on other self, the need of the life, the good, the work of love and sympathy that can truly be done. A realisation of spiritual unity, a dynamisation of the intimate consciousness of one-being, of one self in all beings, can alone found and govern by its truth the action of the divine life.   LD, 1029-30

The law of the divine life is universality in action, organised by an all-seeing Will, with the sense of the true oneness of all.

In the gnostic or divine being, in the gnostic life, there will be a close and complete consciousness of the self of others, a consciousness of their mind, life, physical being which are felt as if they were one's own. The gnostic being will act, not out of a surface sentiment of love and sympathy or any similar feeling, but out of this close mutual consciousness, this intimate oneness. All his action in the world will be enlightened by a truth of vision of what has to be done, a sense of the will of the Divine Reality in him which is also the Divine Reality in others, and it will be done for the Divine in others and the Divine in all, for the effectuation of the truth of purpose of the All as seen in the light of the highest Consciousness and in the way and by the steps through which it must be effectuated in the power of the Supernature. The gnostic being finds himself not only in his own fulfilment, which is the fulfilment of the Divine Being and Will in him, but in the fulfilment of others; his universal individuality effectuates itself in the movement of the All in all beings towards its greater becoming. He sees a divine working everywhere; what goes out from him into the sum of that divine working, from the inner Light, Will, Force that works in him, is his action. There is no separative ego in him to initiate anything; it is the Transcendent and Universal that moves out through his universalised individuality into the action of the universe. As he does not live for a separate ego, so too he does not live for the purpose of any collective ego; he lives in and for the Divine in himself, in and for the Divine in the collectivity, in and for the Divine in all beings. This universality in action, organised by the all-seeing Will in the sense of the realised oneness of all, is the law of his divine living.

It is, then, this spiritual fulfilment of the urge to individual perfection and an inner completeness of being that we mean first when we speak of a divine life. It is the first essential condition of a perfected life on earth, and we are therefore right in making the utmost possible individual perfection our first supreme business. The perfection of the spiritual and pragmatic relation of the individual with all around him is our second preoccupation; the solution of this second desideratum lies in a complete universality and oneness with all life upon earth which is the other concomitant result of an evolution into the gnostic consciousness and nature. But there still remains the third desideratum, a new world, a change in the total life of humanity or, at the least, a new perfected collective life in the earth-nature. This calls for the appearance not only of isolated evolved individuals acting in the unevolved mass, but of many gnostic individuals forming a new kind of beings and a new common life superior to the present individual and common existence.

A spiritual or gnostic being would feel his harmony with the whole gnostic life around him, whatever his position in the whole. According to his place in it he would know how to lead or to rule, but also how to subordinate himself; both would be to him an equal delight: for the Spirit's freedom, because it is eternal, self-existent and inalienable, can be felt as much in service and willing subordination and adjustments with other selves as in power and rule. An inner spiritual freedom can accept its place in the truth of an inner spiritual hierarchy as well as in the truth, not incompatible with it, of a fundamental spiritual equality. It is this self-arrangement of Truth, a natural order of the spirit, that would exist in a common life of different degrees and stages of the evolving gnostic being. Unity is the basis of the gnostic consciousness, mutuality the natural result of its direct awareness of oneness in diversity, harmony the inevitable power of the working of its force. Unity, mutuality and harmony must therefore be the inescapable law of a common or collective gnostic life. What forms it might take would depend upon the will of evolutionary manifestation of the Supernature, but this would be its general character and principle.   LD, 1030-31, 1033

> *New powers of consciousness and new faculties will develop in the gnostic being who will use them in a natural, normal and spontaneous way both for knowledge and for action.*

An evolution of innate and latent but as yet unevolved powers of consciousness is not considered admissible by the modern mind, because these exceed our present formulation of Nature and, to our ignorant preconceptions founded on a limited experience, they seem to belong to the supernatural, to the miraculous and occult; for they surpass the known action of material Energy which is now ordinarily accepted as the sole cause and mode of things and the sole instrumentation of the World-Force. A human working of marvels, by the conscious being discovering and developing an instrumentation of material forces overpassing anything that Nature has herself organised, is accepted as a natural fact and an almost unlimited prospect of our existence; an awakening, a discovery, an instrumentation of powers of consciousness and of spiritual, mental and life forces overpassing anything that Nature or man has yet organised is not admitted as possible. But there would be nothing supernatural or miraculous in such an evolution, except in so far as it would be a supernature or superior nature to ours just as human nature is a supernature or superior nature to that of animal or plant or material objects. Our mind and its powers, our use of reason, our mental intuition and insight, speech, possibilities of philosophical, scientific, aesthetic discovery of the truths and potencies of being and a control of its forces are an evolution that has taken place: yet it would seem impossible if we took our stand on the limited animal consciousness and its capacities; for there is nothing there to warrant so prodigious a progression. But still there are vague initial manifestations, rudimentary elements or arrested possibilities in the animal to which our reason and intelligence with their extraordinary developments stand as an unimaginable journey from a poor and unpromising point of departure. The rudiments of spiritual powers belonging to the gnostic Supernature are similarly there even in our ordinary composition, but only occasionally and sparsely active. It is not irrational to suppose that at this much higher stage of the evolution a similar but greater progression starting from these rudimentary beginnings might lead to another immense development and departure.

In mystic experience, – when there is an opening of the inner centres,[27] or in other ways, spontaneously or by will or endeavour or in the very course of the spiritual growth, – new powers of consciousness have been known to develop; they present themselves as if an automatic consequence of some inner opening or in answer to a call in the being, so much so that it has been found necessary to recommend to the seeker not to hunt after these powers, not to accept or use them. This rejection is logical for those who seek to withdraw from life; for all acceptance of greater power would bind to life or be a burden on the bare and pure urge towards liberation. An indifference to all other aims and issues is natural for the God-lover who seeks God for His own sake and not for power or any other inferior attraction; the pursuit of these alluring but often dangerous forces would be a deviation from his purpose. A similar rejection is a necessary self-restraint and a spiritual discipline for the immature seeker, since such powers may be a great, even a deadly peril; for their supernormality may easily feed in him an abnormal exaggeration of the ego. Power in itself may be dreaded as a temptation by the aspirant to perfection, because power can abase as well as elevate; nothing is more liable to misuse. But when new capacities come as an inevitable result of the growth into a greater consciousness and a greater life and that growth is part of the very aim of the spiritual being within us, this bar does not operate; for a growth of the being into Supernature and its life in Supernature cannot take place or cannot be complete without bringing with it a greater power of consciousness and a greater power of life and the spontaneous development of an instrumentation of knowledge and force normal to that supernature. There is nothing in this future evolution of the being which could be regarded as irrational or incredible; there is nothing in it abnormal or miraculous: it would be the necessary course of the evolution of consciousnesss and its forces in the passage from the mental to the gnostic or supramental formulation of our existence. This action of the forces of Supernature would be a natural, normal and spontaneously simple working of the new higher or greater consciousness into which the being enters in the course of his self-evolution; the gnostic being accepting the gnostic life would develop and use the powers of this greater consciousness, even as man develops and uses the powers of his mental nature.

LD, 1041-43

The life of gnostic beings might fitly be characterised as a superhuman or divine life. But it must not be confused with past and present ideas of supermanhood.

A gnostic Supernature transcends all the values of our normal ignorant Nature; our standards and values are created by ignorance and therefore cannot determine the life of Supernature. At the same time our present nature is a derivation from Supernature and is not a pure ignorance but a half-knowledge; it is therefore reasonable to suppose that whatever spiritual truth there is in or behind its standards and values will reappear in the higher life, not as standards, but as elements transformed, uplifted out of the ignorance and raised into the true harmony of a more luminous existence. As the universalised spiritual individual sheds the limited personality, the ego, as he rises beyond mind to a completer knowledge in Supernature, the conflicting ideals of the mind must fall away from him, but what is true behind them will remain in the life of Supernature. The gnostic consciousness is a consciousness in which all contradictions are cancelled or fused into each other in a higher light of seeing and being, in a unified self-knowledge and world-knowledge. The gnostic being will not accept the mind's ideals and standards; he will not be moved to live for himself, for his ego, or for humanity or for others or for the community or for the State; for he will be aware of something greater than these half-truths, of the Divine Reality, and it is for that he will live, for its will in himself and in all, in a spirit of large universality, in the light of the will of the Transcendence. For the same reason there can be no conflict between self-affirmation and altruism in the gnostic life, for the self of the gnostic being is one with the self of all, – no conflict between the ideal of individualism and the collective ideal, for both are terms of a greater Reality and only in so far as either expresses the Reality or their fulfilment serves the will of the Reality, can they have a value for his spirit. But at the same time what is true in the mental ideals and dimly figured in them will be fulfilled in his existence; for while his consciousness exceeds the human values so that he cannot substitute mankind or the community or the State or others or himself for God, the affirmation of the Divine in himself and a sense of the Divine in others and the sense of oneness with humanity, with all other beings, with all the world because of the Divine in them and a lead towards a greater and better affirmation of the growing Reality in them will be part of his life action. But what he shall do will be decided by the Truth of the Knowledge and Will in him, a total and infinite Truth that is not bound by any single mental law or standard but acts with freedom in the whole reality, with respect for each truth in its place and with a clear knowledge of the forces at work and the intention in the manifesting Divine Nisus at each step of cosmic evolution and in each event and circumstance.

The one rule of the gnostic life would be the self-expression of the Spirit, the will of the Divine Being; that will, that self-expression could manifest through extreme simplicity or through extreme complexity and opulence or in their natural balance, – for beauty and plenitude, a hidden sweetness and laughter in things, a sunshine and gladness of life are also powers and expressions of the Spirit. In all directions the Spirit within determining the law of the nature would determine the frame of the life and its detail and circumstance. In all there would be the same plastic principle; a rigid standardisation, however necessary for the mind's arrangement of things, could not be the law of the spiritual life. A great diversity and liberty of self-expression based on an underlying unity might well become manifest; but everywhere there would be harmony and truth of order.

A life of gnostic beings carrying the evolution to a higher supramental status might fitly be characterised as a divine life; for it would be a life in the Divine, a life of the beginnings of a spiritual divine light and power and joy manifested in material Nature. That might be described, since it surpasses the mental human level, as a life of spiritual and supramental superman-hood. But this must not be confused with past and present ideas of supermanhood; for supermanhood in the mental idea consists of an overtopping of the normal human level, not in kind but in degree of the same kind, by an enlarged personality, a magnified and exaggerated ego, an increased power of mind, an increased power of vital force, a refined or dense and massive exaggeration of the forces of the human Ignorance; it carries also, commonly implied in it, the idea of a forceful domination over humanity by the superman. That would mean a super-manhood of the Nietzschean type; it might be at its worst the reign of the 'blonde beast' or the dark beast or of any and every beast, a return to barbaric strength and ruthlessness and force: but this would be no evolution, it would be a reversion to an old strenuous barbarism.

But earth has had enough of this kind in her past and its repetition can only prolong the old lines; she can get no true profit for her future, no power of self-exceeding, from the Titan, the Asura[28]: even a great or supernormal power in it could only carry her on larger circles of her old orbit. But what has to emerge is something much more difficult and much more simple; it is a self-realised being, a building of the spiritual self, an intensity and urge of the soul and the deliverance and sovereignty of its light and power and beauty, – not an egoistic supermanhood seizing on a mental and vital domination over humanity, but the sovereignty of the Spirit over its own instruments, see its possession of itself and its possession of life in the power of the spirit, a new consciousness in which humanity itself shall find its own self-exceeding and self-fulfilment by the revelation of the divinity that is striving for birth within it. This is the sole true supermanhood and the one real possibility of a step forward in evolutionary Nature.

LD, 1064-65, 1067-68

It would be a misconception to think that a life in the full light of Knowledge would lose its charm and become an insipid monotony. The gnostic manifestation of life would be more full and fruitful and its interest more vivid than the creative interest offered to us by the world of Ignorance.

This new status would indeed be a reversal of the present law of human consciousness and life, for it would reverse the whole principle of the life of the Ignorance. It is for the taste of the Ignorance, its surprise and adventure, one might say, that the soul has descended into the Inconscience and assumed the disguise of Matter, for the adventure and the joy of creation and discovery, an adventure of the Spirit, an adventure of the Mind and Life and the hazardous surprises of their working in Matter, for the discovery and conquest of the new and the unknown; all this constitutes the enterprise of life and all this, it might seem, would cease with the cessation of the Ignorance. Man's life is made up of the light and the darkness, the gains and losses, the difficulties and dangers, the pleasures and pains of the Ignorance, a play of colours moving on a soil of the general neutrality of Matter which has as its basis the nescience and insensibility of the Inconscient. To the normal life-being an existence without the reactions of success and frustration, vital joy and grief, peril and passion, pleasure and pain, the vicissitudes and uncertainties of fate and struggle and battle and endeavour, a joy of novelty and surprise and creation projecting itself into the unknown, might seem to be void of variety and therefore void of vital savour. Any life surpassing these things tends to appear to it as something featureless and empty or cast in the figure of an immutable sameness; the human mind's picture of heaven is the incessant repetition of an eternal monotone. But this is a misconception; for an entry into the gnostic consciousness would be an entry into the Infinite. It would be a self-creation bringing out the Infinite infinitely into form of being, and the interest of the Infinite is much greater and multitudinous as well as more imperishably delightful than the interest of the finite. The evolution in the Knowledge would be a more beautiful and glorious manifestation with more vistas ever unfolding themselves and more intensive in all ways than any evolution could be in the Ignorance. The delight of the Spirit is ever new, the forms of beauty it takes innumerable, its godhead ever young and the taste of delight, *rasa,*[29] of the Infinite eternal and inexhaustible. The gnostic manifestation of life would be more full and fruitful and its interest more vivid than the creative interest of the Ignorance; it would be a greater and happier constant miracle.

If there is an evolution in material Nature and if it is an evolution of being with consciousness and life as its two key-terms and powers, this fullness of being, fullness of consciousness, fullness of life must be the goal of development towards which we are tending and which will manifest at an early or later stage of our destiny. The Self, the Spirit, the Reality that is disclosing itself out of the first inconscience of life and matter, would evolve its complete truth of being and consciousness in that life and matter. It would return to itself, – or, if its end as an individual is to return into its Absolute, it could make that return also, – not through a frustration of life but through a spiritual completeness of itself in life. Our evolution in the Ignorance with its chequered joy and pain of self-discovery and world-discovery, its half-fulfilments, its constant finding and missing, is only our first state. It must lead inevitably towards an evolution in the Knowledge, a self-finding and self-unfolding of the Spirit, a self-revelation of the Divinity in things in that true power of itself in Nature which is to us still a Supernature.

LD, 1068-70

NOTES

*The numbers below refer to the superior figures
after words in the main text.*

1. The principle and support of all existence is the **Self** or **Spirit** (**Atman** or **Brahman** in Sanskrit). From the point of view of the manifested existence, it has three aspects:

a) transcendent: the **Supreme Self** (**Paramatman**), Existence in essence, above the individual and the cosmos, identical with the essential Divine Being, the Supracosmic Reality, the spaceless and timeless Absolute (**Parabrahman**);

b) cosmic: the **Universal Self** (**Atman**), the Spirit manifested in infinite self-extension, the indwelling Spirit equal in all beings;

c) individual: the true **Individual Self** (**Jivatman**): the central being of each living entity, the essential individual consciousness, immutable and free, not affected by desire, ego and ignorance. The Self is one and indivisible notwithstanding its three aspects.

2. To the highest spiritual perception, the One reveals a triple nature: **Existence-Consciousness-Bliss, Sat-Chit-Ananda** (**Sachchidananda**).

In the Supreme the three are not three but one – Existence (**Sat**) is Consciousness (**Chit**), Consciousness is Bliss (**Ananda**). In the superior planes of manifestation, they become triune although inseparable; one can be made more prominent and base or lead the others. In the lower planes they become separable in appearance, though not in their secret reality, and one can exist phenomenally without the others, so that we can speak of an inconscient or a painful existence.

Chit, Consciousness, is not an inert and passive principle; it contains inherently the potential spiritual Energy, **Tapas**, which in the manifestation becomes the dynamic and creative Power or Force, **Shakti. Chit-Tapas** becomes **Chit-Shakti**, the universal Consciousness-Force, the conscious creative Force.

3. The present cosmic manifestation is the result of a double movement: **Involution** and **Evolution**. Involution is a process of self-limitation, of densification, by which the universal Consciousness-Force veils itself by stages until it assumes the appearance of a dense cosmic Inconscience. In this way a series of universal principles, worlds or planes of consciousness have been created, each characterised by certain powers of consciousness.

The three superior planes of this universe are called **the planes of Sachchidananda**. They form universal and fundamental states of the spiritual Reality in which the unity of the Divine Existence, the power of the Divine Consciousness, the bliss of the Divine Delight of existence are put in front. They are far above the reach of normal human consciousness and experience.

Then comes an intermediate plane, called **the Supramental plane**, or the plane of Supermind. It can be characterised as a self-effectuating Truth-Consciousness.

The series of descending planes ends with
– **the mental plane** or plane of Mind,
– **the vital plane** or plane of Life,
– **the physical or material plane**, or plane of Matter.
In the physical plane the involution reaches its last stage in a total Inconscience which becomes the starting point of a gradual evolution. This Inconscience is a stark and utter negation of the Spirit – an indeterminable original chaos, as it were.

In each plane all the powers of consciousness belonging to the planes above it are involved, so that all the powers of the original and universal Consciousness-Force are really involved or hidden even in the Inconscient.

These universal planes are worlds in themselves: they have their own forces, forms and beings. We are partly immersed in them and influenced by them (see Note 6 below), although it is only in the material plane that we have developed sense organs which bring the forces, forms and beings of the world of matter within our normal perception.

Evolution is an opposite process, by which the Consciousness-Force emerges again gradually from the apparent cosmic Inconscience and manifests its hidden powers.

Out of the Inconscient, **Matter** has been organised by the urge of the involved Consciousness-Force and under the pressure of the subtler forces of the physical plane. It has gradually developed into the physical cosmos as we know it. Matter, again by the working of the secret Consciousness-Force and that of the forces of the vital plane above, has produced **Life** and living physical beings: plants and animals. In the animal, once more by a double action, the forces of the mental plane have successfully fashioned an instrument permitting them to come in contact with Matter and organise it: **Mind** is born in the physical world and, with it, Man, the self-conscious thinking animal. The next step of the ascent of the embodied consciousness will be taken under the pressure of the forces from the supramental plane: **Supermind** will emerge in the earthly manifestation. Sri Aurobindo's principal works are a comprehensive study of this new power of consciousness, the conditions of its emergence on earth and the resultant transformation of mankind.

"Mind, Life and Matter are the realised powers of the evolution and wellknown to us; Supermind and the triune aspects of Sachchidananda are the secret principles which are not yet put in front and have still to be realised in the forms of the manifestation and we know them only by hints and a partial and fragmentary action still not disengaged from the lower movements and therefore not easily recognisable." (Sri Aurobindo, *The Life Divine*, p. 664)

It must be noted that, as Sri Aurobindo uses the terms, evolution is not exactly the reverse of involution. Evolution is not a withdrawing, a subtilisation, plane after plane, leading to a reabsorption into the One Unmanifest. It takes place in Matter itself: it is a gradual emergence of higher powers of consciousness, leading to an even greater manifestation of the divine Consciousness-Force *in the material universe*. This is the secret significance of the terrestrial evolution.

4. Man is made up of a temporary surface personality and a deeper eternal soul with an individual Self (Jivatman) presiding from above. The personality has three principal parts; **body, life** and **mind.**

The evolving individual soul is called the **psychic being** by Sri Aurobindo. It stands, so to speak, behind mind, life and body, which are its instruments in the manifestation, and supports them at first in a veiled manner, then, as it grows, more and more openly.

The psychic being is immortal while the body, the vital and the mind are dissolved at death, or a little later. It passes from life to life, gathering the essence of its life experiences and makes that its basis of growth in the evolution of the individual through the ages.

The true central being, the individual Self or Spirit (**Jivatman**) presides over the individual evolution, but it remains above the cosmic manifestation: it is not born nor does it evolve. It puts forward, as a representative of itself, the psychic being, which stands behind the manifestation in mind, life and body, and ensures the continuity of the individual evolution.

The psychic being should not be confused with the vital being which governs the activities of life and is the seat of desires, passions and emotions. The true individual Self should also be distinguished from its distorted reflection, the **ego**. The ego, the little self, which regards itself as separate from others and from the world, is a physical, vital and mental formation; it belongs to the transitory personality and dissolves with it.

5. Mind: in the language of this Yoga the words 'mind' and 'mental' are used to connote specifically that part of the nature which is concerned with cognition and intelligence. It proceeds by the elaboration of images, thoughts, ideas. It has various faculties: intelligence, memory, will, imagination, reason.

The **vital** is the life nature made up of desires, sensations, feelings, passions, energies of action, will of desire, reactions of the desire soul in man and all that play of possessive and other related instincts, anger, fear, greed, lust, etc.

6. The part of our nature of which we are normally conscious is our surface personality, consisting of the body, the (surface) vital and the (surface) mind. But behind this superficial consciousness there exists a far greater, deeper and more powerful consciousness which is in constant touch with the universal planes of Mind, Life and Matter (see Note 3 above). This hidden consciousness which influences and governs us without our knowledge, is sometimes referred to as our **inner being**. Sri Aurobindo differentiates in it three regions or parts. One part is **subconscient**, lower than our waking consciousness; another part is on a level with our waking consciousness but **subliminal**, behind the threshold of consciousness; and yet another is **superconscient**, a higher consciousness above the normal consciousness.

The **subconscient** is a concealed and unexpressed, inarticulate consciousness which works below all our conscious physical activities. It retains the impressions of all our past experiences; not as perceptions, reactions, memories, thoughts, but as a fluid substance of these, as impressions at the same time obscure and obstinate. These impressions can surge up in dream forms as mechanical repetitions, or as 'complexes' which explode in actions and happenings.

The **subliminal** contains, behind the surface mind, an inner mind, larger and more effective; behind the surface vital, an inner vital, larger and more powerful; a subtler physical consciousness behind the surface physical being, more open and plastic and free. And above, the subliminal opens itself to the regions of superconscience, just as it opens below to the subconscient regions.

The **superconscient** contains first certain regions of the mind of which ordinary man is not normally conscious, sources of the higher intuitions and inspirations, then the Supermind and finally that which is above and beyond it (the planes of Sachchidananda).

7. Psychic: that which pertains to the true soul, the 'psyche' or psychic being.

8. The Spirit is the Atman, Brahman, the essential Divine. When the One manifests the Many, that are always inherent in it, it assumes two aspects: **Purusha** and **Prakriti**, the Conscious Being or Soul, and Nature.

The **Purusha** is the true being, or at least represents the true being, on whatever plane it manifests. But in ordinary man, it is covered by the ego and by the ignorant play of the Prakriti, and remains veiled as a 'witness' which upholds and observes the play of the Ignorance. When it emerges, it is perceived at first as a calm, immovable consciousness, detached from the play of Nature. Thereafter it gradually asserts itself as the sovereign Master of Prakriti. Even when it is covered up, it is always present. The emergence of Purusha is the beginning of liberation.

What is commonly meant by **Prakriti** is Nature; it appears to be a play of unconscious and mechanical forces. But behind it is the ever present living Consciousness and Force of the Divine: the divine Shakti. Truly speaking Nature is only the outer or executive aspect of the Shakti or Conscious Force that forms and moves the worlds.

It can be said also that **Nature** is only the lower Prakriti, the Prakriti of mind, life and matter. There exists also a Higher Prakriti (Paraprakriti), the **Supernature** or divine Nature of the Sachchidananda, which has the power of manifesting the Supermind and remains always conscious of the Divine and free from Ignorance and its consequences.

9. Sri Aurobindo calls **Supermind** or **Gnosis** the higher dynamism of spiritual existence. The Supermind is the full Truth-Consciousness in which there can be no place for the principle of division and ignorance. Its fundamental character is knowledge by identity, in which the knower is one with that which is known. It knows the Self, the divine Sachchidananda and also the whole truth of manifestation.

The Supermind possesses an inherent dynamic power of self-determination and self-realisation which sees all and unites all.

10. Dharma: this word, translated variously as 'law', 'moral law', 'duty', 'religion', is used at once in a wide and flexible sense. In its deepest meaning it is 'the law of the action according to the essential nature of each being'. Sri Aurobindo explains this meaning in the last quotation of Chapter IV.

11. Pralaya: is the periodical dissolution of the universe at the end of a cycle of cosmic creation and activity.

12. Tapasya: practice of a discipline, and generally of austerities for a determined end; spiritual effort, concentration of the energies in a spiritual discipline or process.

13. Rishi: 'one who sees (the Truth)', a seer, a sage.

Yoga: union with the Divine; the discipline by which one seeks deliberately and consciously to realise this union, or more generally, to attain to a higher consciousness.

Yogi: one who practises yoga; one who has attained the goal of yoga.

14. The **Bhagavad-Gita** (The Celestial Song): an episode in the ancient epic Mahabharata in which, on the battlefield of Kurukshetra, the Divine, in the form of Sri Krishna, gives his teachings to Arjuna. It is the most famous of the Indian Scriptures and universally revered.

15. Swami Vivekananda: (born and died in Bengal, 1863-1902): one of the chief disciples of Sri Ramakrishna and founder of the Ramakrishna Mission.

16. Nirvana: dissolution of the separate individual self (the little self, the ego); extinction of all separative consciousness, of desire and egoistic action and mentality; it is not necessarily the extinction of all being, but of being as we know it.

17. Whether for the individual or the collectivity, Sri Aurobindo stresses the fundamental difference which exists between the true **Self**, immutable and free, one with the supreme **Self**, and the **ego**, a transient separative individual consciousness identified with the mind, vital and physical, open and more or less subject to the forces of all kinds belonging to these planes.

In the evolution, the ego has a role of protection; it is necessary as long as the individual is not conscious of the true Self. But it becomes unnecessary when the psychic being, which is a delegate of the true Self, openly asserts itself, and in order that the psychic being may take possession of the nature, the ego has to abdicate and disappear.

18. Ishwara, the Divine as Lord and Master of the universe, and **Shakti**, the conscious creative Power, form of a fundamental duality somewhat different from the **Purusha-Prakriti** duality (see Note 8, above). Purusha and Prakriti are separate powers, while Ishwara and

Shakti are contained in each other. Ishwara is Purusha who contains Prakriti and rules by the power of the Shakti within him. Shakti is Prakriti ensouled by Purusha and acts by the will of the Ishwara, whose presence in her movements she carries always with her.

The Shakti of the Ishwara (**Ishwari-Shakti**) is the divine **Consciousness-Force** or **World-Mother**, who contains all and carries all within herself, and to manifest it in Time and Space is her role. She thus appears as the mediatrix between the eternal One and the manifested Many.

These two dualities, as also the third fundamental duality **Brahman-Maya**, correspond to different spiritual experiences or realisations in Yoga (see *The Synthesis of Yoga* Part II, Chapter IV, and *The Life Divine*, Vol. II, Chapter II).

19. Bhakti: is devotion, a **bhakta** is one who follows the path of devotion, a devotee, a worshipper.

20. Between the thinking mind and the Supermind there are a number of ranges, planes or layers of consciousness in which the element or substance of mind and consequently its movements also become more and more illumined and powerful and wide.

The **Overmind** is the highest of these intervening ranges; it is full of lights and powers; but from the point of view of what is above it, it is the line of the soul's turning away from the complete and indivisible Knowledge and its descent towards Ignorance. For although it draws from the Truth, it is here that begins the separation of the aspects of the Truth and their working out as if they were independent truths and forces, and this is a process that ends, as one descends to ordinary mind, life and matter, in a complete division, fragmentation, separation from the indivisible Truth above.

It is from the Overmind that all the different arrangements of the creative Truth of things originate. Out of the Overmind they come down to the **intuitive mind** and are transmitted from it to the **illumined mind** and the **higher mind** to be arranged there for our intelligence. But they lose more and more of their power and certitude and harmony in the transmission as they come down to the lower levels.

The Overmind is the world of the great Gods, the divine Creators. One can consider it as the line separating the higher self of the Universe of Consciousness from the lower half. The **Higher Hemisphere** consists of the planes of **Sat, Chit, Ananda, Mahas** (the **Supermind**); the **Lower Hemisphere** of **Mind, Life** and **Matter**.

In the individual yoga, as in the collective evolution, consciousness has to rise successively to each of the ranges extending from the thinking mind to the Supermind. In the passages quoted in Chapter VII, Sri Aurobindo describes the characteristic functioning of the consciousness on these levels.

21. Mantra: "the word that reveals", a combination of words or sounds having a spiritual significance and power. The function of a mantra is to create in the consciousness vibrations which will prepare it for the realisation of what the mantra symbolises and is supposed to carry within itself.

22. Brahman: the supreme Reality, the Absolute, the Divine (see Note 1, above).

23. The Trinities of the Spirit: the fundamental Trinities have been mentioned in Notes 1 and 2.

"The Transcendent, the Universal, the Individual are three powers overarching, underlying and penetrating the whole manifestation; this is the first of the Trinities. In the unfolding of consciousness also, these are the three fundamental terms and none of them can be neglected if we would have the experience of the whole Truth of existence." (*The Synthesis of Yoga*, p. 247)

"A trinity of transcendent existence, self-awareness and self-delight (*Sachchidananda*) is, indeed, the metaphysical description of the supreme Atman, the self-formulation, to our awakened knowledge, of the Unknowable whether conceived as a pure Impersonality or as a cosmic Personality manifesting the universe." (*The Synthesis of Yoga*, pp. 12-13)

24. Idea: term belonging to the Platonic vocabulary where it designates the essential form or type of things, a kind of eternal and immutable model. The Idea to Plato is the true reality; all the rest is an appearance or a derivative.

The **Real-Idea** is a perception of truth which contains in itself the force of its own realisation.

Sri Aurobindo distinguishes the Idea, which belongs to the higher regions of the mind (see Note 20), from the Real-Idea, which belongs to the Supermind. The Idea and the Will-Force are separated, whereas the Real-Idea possesses in itself the spiritual dynamism inherent in the higher Reality, the Supernature. But Sri Aurobindo uses sometimes the word Idea, meaning thereby Real-Idea.

25. Vedanta: originally the word Vedanta meant "the end or culmination of the Vedas" and refers to the Upanishads; subsequently, one of the six classical schools of the Hindu philosophy, which based itself on the Upanishads, also came to be known as Vedanta or Later Vedanta.

26. Swadharma: the law of action proper to an individual (see Note 10 above). **Swabhava**: the distinctive nature of each being.

27. The **inner centres** are the seven lotuses or psychological centres (**chakras**) of the subtle body. They become active in the course of yoga and connect the waking consciousness to the subtler, deeper or higher states of consciousness.

28. Asuras: hostile beings or forces belonging to the vital mind plane. The traditional legends of India speak of them as Sons of Darkness, and later, as giants, titans or demons.

29. Rasa: the sap, the juice, the inner savour of things; essential delight, principle or aesthetic or spiritual enjoyment.

REFERENCES

The source of each text is indicated at its end in an abbreviated form. The titles are abbreviated:

> LD – *The Life Divine*
> HC – *The Human Cycle*
> SY – *The Synthesis of Yoga*

The page numbers following the title abbreviation refer to the Sri Aurobindo Birth Centenary Library edition and its impressions. (*The Human Cycle* is included in the Centenary Library volume entitled *Social and Political Thought*.)

BIBLIOGRAPHICAL NOTE

THE LIFE DIVINE

The Life Divine first appeared in the monthly journal *Arya*, its fifty-two original chapters being published in fifty-four instalments between August 1914 and January 1919. In 1939 and 1940 Sri Aurobindo revised and enlarged these chapters preparatory to the publication of the work in book form by the Arya Publishing House, Calcutta. The twenty-eight chapters which make up Book One, published in November 1939 as "Volume I", include the first twenty-seven chapters from the *Arya* (with the same titles and in the same order) and, in addition, a twenty-eighth chapter which is entirely new. With the exception of Chapter XIX and Chapter XXIII, both of which received major additions and changes, the revision of the chapters of Book One was confined to the alternation and addition of marks of punctuation, words or short passages.

The first edition of Book Two, "recast and enlarged", was published in July 1940 as "Volume II", in two parts bound separately. Among its twenty-eight chapters twelve were included that were entirely new: Chapters I, II, V, VI, X, XIV, XXIII, XXIV, XXV, XXVI, XXVII and XXVIII. Of the remaining sixteen chapters, eleven, namely Chapters III, IV, VII, VIII, IX, XI, XII, XIII, XVII, XIX and XX, were similar to *Arya* chapters; nevertheless all of them were substantially revised and several were given new titles. Chapters XV, XVI, XVIII, XXI and XXII contain some material from the *Arya*, but much that was entirely new. Chapters XVIII and XXI were so thoroughly revised that they may be considered new.

The Arya Publishing House published a second edition of Book One as "Volume I" in 1943 and a second edition of Book Two, Parts I and II, bound together, as "Volume II", in 1944. These second editions incorporate a few minor corrections and changes by the author. A third edition of Book One was published only as "Volume I" by the Arya Publishing House in 1947.

The first American edition of *The Life Divine* was published in 1949 by the Sri Aurobindo Library, New York. A second impression of this edition was issued by the same publisher in 1951, and a third impression by the India Library Society, New York, in 1965. In all these impressions the two books were combined in a single volume, and a comprehensive index was provided.

The Sri Aurobindo International Centre of Education, Pondicherry, published two impressions of the fourth Indian edition of *The Life Divine*, both complete in one volume, in 1955 and 1960. The fifth edition was published by the Sri Aurobindo Ashram, Pondicherry, in 1970. Three impressions were issued that year. The first formed part of the deluxe edition of the Sri Aurobindo Birth Centenary Library, Book One and Book Two, Part I comprising Volume 18, and Book Two, Part II comprising Volume 19 of the set. The second impression constituted the corresponding volumes of the popular edition of the Centenary Edition, a facsimile reproduction of the deluxe edition. The third impression was reproduced similarly in two volumes but in a reduced format. The fourth impression (1973) was identical to the third, except that it included a glossary of Sanskrit terms and two appendixes. The fifth and sixth impressions (1977 and 1980) incorporated a few corrections of typographical and editorial errors and included a new index and glossary. The fifth impression was in two volumes; the sixth was bound as one.

The seventh impression (1982), like the five preceding impressions, was reproduced by photo-offset from the fifth edition (1970), the deluxe Centenary Edition. It incorporated for the first time a few minor corrections made by the author in his copy of the 1940 edition. The eighth impression (1987) is identical to the seventh.

THE HUMAN CYCLE

The first edition of *The Human Cycle* published in 1949 by the Sri Aurobindo Ashram, Pondicherry, contained the following note written by the author and dated November 1949:

"The chapters constituting this book were written under the title *The Psychology of Social Development* from month to month in the philosophical monthly, *Arya*, from August 15, 1916 to July 15, 1918 and used recent and contemporary events as well as illustrations from the history of the past in its explanation of the theory of social evolution put forward in these pages. The reader has therefore to go back in his mind to the events of that period in order to follow the line of thought and the atmosphere in which it developed. At one time a suggestion was made to bring this part up to date, especially with some reference to later developments in Nazi Germany and the development of a totalitarian Communist regime in Russia. But afterwards it was felt that there was sufficient prevision and allusion to these events, and more elaborate description or criticism of them was not essential. There was, even without them, an adequate working out and elucidation of this theory of the social cycle."

The *Arya* text of the work was revised by Sri Aurobindo before the publication of the first edition. It was at this time that the title of the book was changed, and chapter titles, which were lacking in the *Arya*, were provided. The revision, which was light throughout, was more substantial in Chapters XIII, XVI-XX, XXIII and XXIV. New passages of some length were added to Chapters XVI and XIX.

An edition of *The Human Cycle*, textually identical to the first, was published by the Sri Aurobindo Library, New York, in 1950. This edition contained an index.

Since 1962 *The Human Cycle* has been printed along with *The Ideal of Human Unity* and *War and Self-Determination*. Five editions of this combined edition have been published.

The 1977 edition of *The Human Cycle* is the first separate edition of the book to be brought out since 1950. It is reproduced by photo-offset from the second combined edition, and includes a new index and glossary.

THE SYNTHESIS OF YOGA

The Synthesis of Yoga first appeared serially in the monthly review *Arya*, beginning from its first issue, August 1914. Seventy-two chapters, preceded by five introductory chapters, had been issued by January 1921 when the journal ceased publication, leaving the series incomplete.

In 1948 the first eleven chapters of the *Arya* text, extensively revised, enlarged, and expanded into twelve chapters, were published as *The Synthesis of Yoga: Part I*, "The Yoga of Divine Works", by the Sri Aurobindo Library, Madras. This identical text was reissued by the Sri Aurobindo Ashram, Pondicherry, in a second edition in 1953. The same text had been separately published in 1950 by the Sri Aurobindo Library, New York, as *The Synthesis of Yoga, Book One*. This American edition included an index and a glossary.

In 1955 the Sri Aurobindo International University Centre, Pondicherry, published the first combined edition of *The Synthesis of Yoga* as Volume IV of its collection of Sri Aurobindo's works under the title, *On Yoga I: The Synthesis of Yoga*. All available chapters of the book, revised or unrevised, were included in this edition, the text of which has been used as the text of all subsequent editions. The five introductory chapters are reprinted from the *Arya* text. Chapters I to XII are taken from the 1948 edition and to these twelve chapters is added an incomplete thirteenth from the manuscripts of the author to make up Part I, "The Yoga of Divine Works". Part II, "The Yoga of Integral Knowledge" forms chapters XIII to XL of the *Arya* text. (These chapters were revised slightly by the author.) Parts III and IV, entitled here "The Yoga of Divine Love" and "The Yoga of Self-Perfection", comprise the remaining chapters of the *Arya* series.

It should be noted that although this text is complete insofar as it includes all available material, *The Synthesis of Yoga* as a whole was never completed. Not only was the "Yoga of Self-Perfection" left unfinished, but a proposed additional section was not begun. It should also be remembered that only the first part, "The Yoga of Divine Works", was issued during Sri Aurobindo's lifetime in a thoroughly revised form. The second and more especially the third and fourth parts must be considered as belonging to an earlier period.

A second impression of the first combined edition was issued by the S.A.I.I.C. in 1957. In 1965 the Sri Aurobindo International Centre of Education, Pondicherry, brought out a second edition. The third and fourth editions (1970) entitled simply *The Synthesis of Yoga*, comprised Volumes 20 and 21 of the *Sri Aurobindo Birth Centenary Library*, deluxe and popular editions respectively. The popular edition was a facsimile reproduction of the deluxe edition. The fifth edition was similarly reproduced, but in an abbreviated format. There were two impressions of this edition (1971 and 1973), both of which were issued by the Sri Aurobindo Ashram Trust, Pondicherry.

The text of the sixth edition (1988) is the same as that of the fifth, excepting a few corrections of minor, mostly typographical errors. The addition of an index constitutes a new edition.

Sri Aurobindo
Rebirth and Karma

REBIRTH AND KARMA by Sri Aurobindo
In depth study of the concepts of rebirth, karma and the higher lines of karma. One of the best introductions to this area we've ever found.
LOTUS PRESS   ISBN 0-941524-63-9   190 pp pb $9.95

THE LIFE DIVINE by Sri Aurobindo
The Life Divine is Sri Aurobindo's major philosophical exposition, spanning more than a thousand pages and integrating the major spiritual directions of mankind into a coherent picture of the growth of the spiritual essence of man through diverse methods, philosophies and spiritual practices.
LOTUS PRESS   ISBN 0-941524-62-0   1113 pp pb $39.95
LOTUS PRESS   ISBN 0-941524-61-2   1113 pp pb $29.95

Sri Aurobindo
The Life Divine

Sri Aurobindo
The Integral Yoga
Sri Aurobindo's Teaching and Method of Practice

THE INTEGRAL YOGA
Sri Aurobindo's Teaching and Method of Practice
by Sri Aurobindo (compilation)
> "These carefully selected excerpts from the writings of Sri Aurobindo provide a wonderfully accessible entre into the writings of one of the great masters of spiritual synthesis."
> Ram Dass

LOTUS PRESS   ISBN 0-941524-76-0   416 pp pb $14.95

SYNTHESIS OF YOGA, US EDITION by Sri Aurobindo
In *The Synthesis of Yoga* Sri Aurobindo unfolds his vision of an integral yoga embracing all the powers and activities of man. First, he reviews the three great yogic paths of Knowledge, Works and Love, along with Hatha Yoga, Raja Yoga and Tantra, and then integrates them all into a great symphony. "Truth of philosophy is of a merely theoretical value unless it can be lived, and we have therefore tried in the *The Synthesis of Yoga* to arrive at a synthetical view of the principles and methods of the various lines of spiritual self-discipline and the way in which they can lead to an integral divine life in the human existence".

Sri Aurobindo
The Synthesis of Yoga

LOTUS PRESS   ISBN 0-941524-66-3   899 pp hb $34.95
LOTUS PRESS   ISBN 0-941524-65-5   899 pp pb $29.95

Available from your local bookseller or
Lotus Press, PO Box 325, Twin Lakes, WI 53181 • 262-889-8561
www.lotuspress.com • email: lotuspress@lotuspress.com

Sri Aurobindo
Secret of the Veda

SECRET OF THE VEDA by Sri Aurobindo

In this ground-breaking book, Sri Aurobindo has revealed the secret of the Veda and illustrated his method with numerous translations of the ancient hymns. *Secret of the Veda* has been acclaimed by scholars and yogins as the ultimate key to revealing the hidden sense and secret inner meanings of the original spiritual revelation of the Veda. The *Rig Veda* provides an inner spiritual and psychological practice to achieve realization. It is the foundation upon which the Upanishads were later developed. *Now in its first US edition.*

LOTUS PRESS   ISBN 0-914955-19-5   581 pp   pb $19.95

ESSAYS ON THE GITA by Sri Aurobindo

Sri Aurobindo
Essays on the Gita

The *Bhagavad Gita* stands alone in the spiritual tradition of humanity by being at the same time a Scripture, a teaching , a poetic utterance and a practical guidebook to the problems of life in the world. For this reason, the Gita is a powerful aid to anyone who wants to integrate the life of the Spirit with the issues of life in the world. It does not "cut the knot" but systematically works to untie it. In so doing, it helps us clarify the issues alive within ourselves. Sri Aurobindo understood these issues and in his famous *Essays on the Gita* he was able to reveal many subtle and hidden aspects of the teaching of the Gita. He entered into the spirit of the original and created a commentary that has stood the test of time in its lucidity and value for anyone wishing to truly understand the *Bhagavad Gita*. *Essays on the Gita* has been widely acclaimed for opening up the deeper sense of the *Bhagavad Gita*. *Now in its first US edition.*

LOTUS PRESS   ISBN 0-914955-18-7   588 pp   pb $19.95

Sri Aurobindo
The Mother

THE MOTHER by Sri Aurobindo

Sri Aurobindo has created, in this small book, a powerful guide to the practice of spirituality in life. To discover this gem is to gain a constant companion whose guidance remains forever meaningful. Its power of expression and meaning are so concentrated and far reaching that many have called it "Matri Upanishad", the Upanishad of the Mother. Sri Aurobindo's Matri Upanishad is the text which reveals this power and energy of creation in its universal and personal sense, providing both truth of philosophy and truth of yogic experience at one and the same time. *Now in its first US edition.*

LOTUS PRESS   ISBN 0-941524-79-5   62 pp   pb $2.95

SAVITRI: A LEGEND AND A SYMBOL by Sri Aurobindo

Sri Aurobindo
Savitri
A Legend and a Symbol

Savitri is an inner guidebook for the soul. These mantric verses imbue even the body with potent spiritual resonance. In this epic spiritual poem, Sri Aurobindo reveals his vision of mankind's destiny within the universal evolution. He sets forth the optimistic view that life on earth has a purpose, and he places our travail within the context of this purpose: to participate in the evolution of consciousness that represents the secret thread behind life on earth. Sri Aurobindo's verses describe the origin of the universe, the appearance of sentient beings and the stages of evolution, as well as speak to many of mankind's unanswered questions concerning pain and death. *Now in its first US edition.*

LOTUS PRESS   ISBN 0-941524-80-9   816 pp   pb $24.95

Available from your local bookseller or
Lotus Press, PO Box 325, Twin Lakes, WI 53181 • 262-889-8561
www.lotuspress.com • email: lotuspress@lotuspress.com

OTHER TITLES BY SRI AUROBINDO

Available from your local bookseller or
LOTUS PRESS, Box 325, Twin Lakes, WI 53181 USA
262/889-8561 • www. lotuspress.com
email: lotuspress@lotuspress.com